NEGATIVE STRESS IS THE
GREAT DISEASE OF WESTERN CULTURE.
GET THE CURE WITH . . .

THE PORTABLE PROBLEM SOLVER

Discover . . .

- How Western culture's "Doing" Model creates a stressful, unbalanced life that is driven by work and ignores play

- How obsession with outward physical appearance is more than a stressor—and can damage your internal growth

- What two things in the world, and ONLY two things, you have absolute control over

- How the Eastern Model of "Being" will dramatically reduce your stress

- Why money does not solve problems, but instead creates them

- How to get off the never-ending treadmill of wanting, getting, and wanting more

- Why your mental health depends on your ability to live in the moment

- What seven simple steps will allow you to cope with—and grow from—*any* problem

Also by Susanna McMahon

The Portable Problem Solver:
Having Healthy Relationships

The Portable Therapist

The Portable
Problem Solver

Coping with Life's Stressors

Susanna McMahon, Ph.D.

A Dell Trade Paperback

A DELL TRADE PAPERBACK

Published by
Dell Publishing
a division of
Bantam Doubleday Dell Publishing Group, Inc.
1540 Broadway
New York, New York 10036

Library of Congress Cataloging-in-Publication Data

McMahon, Susanna.
    The portable problem solver: coping with life's stressors/by Susanna McMahon.
        p.   cm.
    ISBN 0-440-50735-9
    1. Stress (Psychology) 2. Stress management. 3. Life change events.
    4. Problem solving. 5. Self-help techniques. I. Title.
    RC455.4.S87M36   1996
    155.9'042—dc20   95-46839
                                                                   CIP

Printed in the United States of America

Published simultaneously in Canada

August 1996

10 9 8 7 6 5 4 3 2 1

BVG

This book is dedicated to:

The pilgrims—my clients;
The angels—my friends; and
The heroes—my mentors.

It was written for everyone who
struggles to make sense of it all.

The biggest problem in the world could have been solved when it was small.
> —WITTER BYNNER
>> *The Way of Life According to Lao Tzu*

A hero is defined as the person who can solve a problem that other people can't.
> —M. SCOTT PECK
>> *Further Along The Road Less Traveled*

↶ Contents

↝ Acknowledgments

I do not believe that any book can ever be written without great help and input from others. Because this book deals with the issues in life that cause stress and create problems, the ideas presented here are dependent upon my experiences and relationships with others. For this reason I need to acknowledge my world—everyone that I have ever known—because in varying degrees everyone has influenced me. Let me be the first to admit that nothing I know or write is completely original and that, as a psychologist and author, I think of myself as a collector of information and a compiler of stories. Everyone has an interesting and informative story to tell, but the people I am most intimate with naturally have the stories that influence me the most.

First of all, I want to thank every client I have worked with. Each of you has taught me much more than I have given back. Above all, you have shown me that we are all pilgrims of life— we all painfully struggle to find the path. Just as the actual pilgrims during medieval times suffered and experienced great deprivations and pain in their quest to reach their sacred place, so, too, do we experience similar difficulties in our journeys. I am most appreciative to all of you for sharing with me and trusting me with your most intimate stories.

My friends are truly the angels in my life, for just as angels help and support us and make themselves known in our most difficult times, so also are my close friends there for me. You know who you are and that I love you all and thank you beyond measure.

The heroes in my life have been my mentors—those wise, loving, and supportive beings that function as role models and enlightened teachers. First there is Timothy—my life partner and greatest ally in my struggle. He is a hero because he demonstrates unsung courage and the most loving heart that I have ever known. My other great love is Buzz, who has been my mentor and teacher from the beginning. All that I practice, believe, and write started with him and his Natural High theory. When I was a graduate student, Len Ullmann taught me the importance of separating myself from my work and my achievements—this has been a lifetime lesson for which I am forever grateful. Wendy Ullmann taught me that no matter what is happening, I can cope; everyone needs to have such a friend and mentor. Other mentors have been Jon Krapfl, Roger Maley, Marco Mariotto, Gordon and Jo Paul, and Tom Powers—to all of them I owe more than I can say. However, none of the above are in any way responsible for what I have done with what they taught me. Thus this book does not reflect their ideas or concepts; rather, the fact that I wrote it does.

My family functions at different times as pilgrims, angels, and heroes. They provide my greatest challenges and my supreme joys, often at the same time. My story is enriched by all of them and I thank them with great love.

There are so many others who have enhanced my life, but listing them would require another book. This book would not be possible without the encouragement and support of my agent, Margret McBride, and her staff, and my editors at Dell, Trish Todd and Eric Wybenga. Thank you so much for believing in me and making it happen.

ᑐ *Introduction*

You know that life is stressful and problematic. No one escapes having problems; no one is immune to stress. These are basic realities for all of us. I developed the ideas that form this book from learning to cope with my own stressors and then encouraging my clients to do the same. Early in my clinical training I realized that there is an infinite number of symptoms and difficulties and it is easy to become overwhelmed by their variety. The process of problem-solving life's stressors begins by classifying problems into a relatively small number of categories and then developing coping strategies that can be effectively used in all situations. I also realized that all of us are constantly dealing with one or another of these types of problems; the actual process of living means dealing with difficulties. No one can change this reality and no one is exempt from the process. Perhaps, then, many of our problems are necessary because they become the catalysts for our developmental growth.

Others—much wiser than I—had already discovered that one of the core attributes of good therapy is to replace the perception of being overwhelmed by a problem with the recognition of the challenge involved in overcoming the difficulty. By doing so you discover the vast array of problem-solving skills and strategies at your disposal. Therapy involves both the provision of support and the retraining necessary to recognize and utilize resources and attributes in a constructive manner. All of us, including you, are natural problem solvers, but you may forget this innate talent when you are in the midst of pain and change. You have the potential to cope with great difficulties and to perceive your problems as challenges. When you are doing well, when things in your life are working, you will more easily recognize these abilities. But when your problems overwhelm you and things start falling apart around you, you will probably forget your skills and stop trusting in your natural abilities. It is at these times that you may reach out for help with your struggle, your difficulties, your problematic life.

At some time or other everyone feels lost, vulnerable, and unable to cope. Everyone feels pain and suffers. It is exactly for these reasons that I believe problems are necessary and instructive. But this may not be what you have been trained to believe. Probably you learned that being successful means being happy and not having any problems. This concept of success and happiness is a myth similar to the one that having the right person love you will solve all your difficulties. I feel very blessed in my profession because being a therapist has allowed me to burst such myths and illusions quickly. Working with many so-called successful individuals has taught me that external success can create more problems than it solves. The highly desired state of the problem-free life simply does not exist. But this does not mean that you should give up and allow your problems to overwhelm you. Rather it means that you will need to live the reality rather than dream about the illusion. Life itself means having problems; the process of living means dealing with your problems.

This book is not about the basic problems of existence: finding food, clothing, and shelter and surviving on a day-to-day basis. Such difficulties are not those presented in therapy, nor are they discussed here. Instead this book will deal with what I call luxury problems—the difficulties encountered once you have satisfied your basic needs. Perhaps many who live in poverty cannot imagine that tremendous problems can still exist once a state of comfort has been achieved and that great unhappiness often coexists with luxury and affluence. While it is true that comfort and wealth solve the problems of physical existence, it is also true that they do not satisfy emotional or spiritual needs. Instead a state of luxury allows one to focus on internal unrest because it removes the distraction of physical discomfort. In other words once the problems of existence have been resolved, you move up what Abraham Maslow called the hierarchy of needs and discover the emotional and spiritual problems.

I originally envisioned *The Portable Problem Solver* as one long book dealing with both relationships and life's stressors. The problems encountered with family, lovers, friends, sexuality, colleagues, and community are at times all-encompassing and worthy of being a separate book. For help in coping with relationship problems I refer you to *The Portable Problem Solver: Having Healthy Relationships*. The nonrelationship issues in life that cause great stress—work, money, time, changes and choices, beliefs and biases, disease and disorders, and loss and death—are discussed in the present book. The common thread in both books is found in the seven problem-solving steps, which have been designed to teach you to become an active and aware problem solver. Most importantly they will help you recognize that the skills needed to solve one type of difficulty will also work with all problems. This means that once you have learned to use these steps and resolved any one problem, you will have mastered the ability to be a problem solver in all situations.

Because you are a survivor—you are living, coping, learning, and growing—you have already solved many problems on your own and have used problem-solving skills, perhaps without being completely aware of what you were doing. By discovering the seven steps and consciously using them to work through your current problems, you will learn to recognize your skills and simultaneously alleviate your fear of future difficulties. The goal of *The Portable Problem Solver* is to change your perception from that of being overwhelmed by your problems into the recognition of their importance for your development, thereby creating the awareness that you can cope. No matter what happens, you will be able to deal with it. I hope that you will learn to perceive your difficulties as challenges and to face them with confidence. I like to compare therapy with learning to use a toolbox; the tools are the resources and skills you need to build your life. You have the resources to be a problem solver. The problem-solving steps are effective tools, and this book tells you how to use them constructively.

Each of you has your own story to tell—a life story composed of your personal responses and reactions to all the difficulties you have encountered. The more stories you tell, the better storyteller you become. Likewise the more problems you have worked through, the more practiced you have become in the art of problem solving. Where you are at this moment is a function of your ability to solve, resolve, accept, or overcome your multitude of past problems. When you reflect back on your life, you can probably see how helpful or important these conflicts have been; you will recognize that you have learned what you needed to know in order to move on. It is only when you look ahead and imagine what your future problems will be that you may become fearful. Perhaps the important lesson here is to realize that you can cope, you will prevail, and you will continue to learn and grow. There is a finite number of problems, but there is an infinite number of variations on these problems. Each one of you will take a problem and make it unique by adding your own details, experiences, and reactions. You are continually in the process of writing your own life story. The details are different for each of you, but the nature of each problem is universal because all of your conflicts are human ones and therefore shared by others. The recognition of this allows you to understand and empathize with others. It creates your human capacity to care and to love. Your challenges lead you to the necessity of going within and learning about your internal self. This discovery leads to being the best you can be for yourself.

In my first book, *The Portable Therapist,* the concepts of weak ego (the need to be esteemed by others and from the externals in life), self-esteem (the ability to love and recognize the worth and value within the self), and the importance of feeling universal belongingness were discussed. You were trained on a linear, competitive, perfectionistic, work-related model, the Doing model; what this society does not teach is how to *Be,* the Being model. This book takes these constructs to the next level and attempts to show how they impact upon your day-to-day activities. In reality there is probably only one core human problem: insecurity. When you are insecure, you will look to the external things in life to help make you feel secure. When you find things that do this, you cling to them and often become dependent on them for your feelings of worth and security. This process, known as attachment, provides you with short-term security and long-term difficulty. All attachments eventually cause problems. The only way ultimately to resolve these problems is to become internally secure—to love your Self and generate your own self-worth. Then you can begin to detach—to let go—of others, things, and even finally life itself. But you cannot detach until you have first attached. Therefore there is no way around it: You will always be coping with some difficulty or another. You will always be practicing your problem-solving skills. How wonderful that you already possess what you need—experience, potential, and the desire to change. You already have the makings of the hero, the great problem solver. I hope this book helps you recognize your heroic capabilities. I hope it en-courages you (gives you courage) because, God knows, all of us need as much courage as possible in the struggle to make sense of this crazy world and to be heroic in this problematic process called life.

Work is love made visible.

—KAHLIL GIBRAN

I ⤳ Work

One of the greatest stressors we all share is work. At some time all of us have been overwhelmed, miserable, and dissatisfied because of work-related issues. One of the reasons for this is that in this society work has taken on a much greater meaning than simply what we do in order to survive. Cross-cultural research consistently shows that Americans tend to think of work as a means of achieving status, power, and control. These attributes are much more valued, and attainable, in this culture than in many others. As a result other cultures seem to "work in order to live," whereas Americans seem to "live in order to work." Management studies also indicate that the United States views status as a function of achievement: Our worth comes from our work. One of the most striking differences between work in this culture and others, and one that is most relevant to this discussion, is the impact that work has on the overall quality of life.

For example it is common in this country to work all day, run some errands, watch some TV, and fall into bed exhausted, but feeling satisfied that we have been productive. We have achieved something. By this measure weekends and vacations, rather than being a respite from work, are a "downtime" in which we worry about what we will have to do once back at work. Many of us get upset when we are not producing, achieving, or working; we have a hard time relaxing. Therefore it is not uncommon to take our work along on weekends or vacations in order to alleviate the discomfort of nonproductive periods. We may realize that this behavior is somewhat dysfunctional, but it does feel more comfortable than being idle. Relaxing, "being," and letting go are not taught to us in our work ethos; we have learned to resist not doing something, not being productive.

Losing the Balance

Thus the balance between work and play seems to lean heavily toward work in this country. Not enough attention is given to play. This results in an unbalanced life and the unnecessary stressors that occur when there is a preoccupation with only one end of the continuum. In this culture work often provides the significant, and sometimes total, meaning for adult life. This is not the case in all cultures; many European and Eastern countries do not equate work with status or worth. At this point we might retort, "But the Protestant work ethic came from Europe. The pilgrims and early settlers were transplanted Europeans." And we would be absolutely correct. However, we need to remember that for the most part our early settlers were not representative of a cross section of European society. They were frequently the outcasts of their society, or self-exiled, and therefore often desperate people with very little to lose. Faith and hard work kept them alive and led to the popular ethic that if we believe in ourselves and work hard enough, we can accomplish the impossible—or at the very least become outwardly successful. From this developed the idea that hard work is the path to success and status—the Horatio Alger concept of life. And for all generations until the present, Americans have honored the merits of this concept. Each successive generation seems to have grown more successful, materialistic, and obsessed with work.

At some time in the present century life in this culture lost any semblance of balance and became driven by work. We began to think of all aspects of life in terms of work: sports, school, education, relationships, having a hobby, self-improvement, even living well all became "hard work." We have even learned to perceive appearance as something we must "work on." It seems that everything we do is discussed in terms of work. Things once perceived as normal and natural life stages are now viewed as work. Having relationships, raising children, learning, growing, and aging are no longer perceived as part of the natural process of life, but are considered in terms of effort and the amount of work we must expend. Even our life stages are not immune: Childhood is perceived as difficult work, having or being an adolescent is an "impossible job," and adulthood is viewed as the stage in which we must work on ourselves, get ahead, and achieve our goals. We start working on our retirement (emotionally and financially) when we are still young; when we actually do retire, we then begin working on getting ready to die. After all, dying well is even considered an effort. Thus there is no longer any part of our lives that is not perceived as work.

The Doing Model

This is madness! All of this work is interfering with our lives. It would be difficult to imagine any "normal" American reading the foregoing without relating to some part of it. And yet we do not have to feel defensive or try to take all the blame for being workaholics or uncomfortable when we are not working. We have received excellent, if unfortunate, training on how to be successful. This training can be conceptualized as a "model"—a covert guide for living in Western society. We can picture this model as a straight line and can label the beginning as birth, and the end, not death but retirement. This is because the model is only concerned with doing in order to achieve; in this work-dominated society, achieving ceases when we retire. It is not coincidental that if we were to place death on the model, it would usually occur very soon after retirement. Most of us are familiar with the statistics of workaholics and overachievers and what happens when they do retire.

If we were to observe this model from the beginning and continue it throughout our social development, we would clearly see the goals and achievements needed to define external success: an education in "good" schools starting with elementary school or even preschool; a degree, or even an advanced degree from a reputable university; a good job with a prestigious firm; quick and steady promotions and raises; marriage or a stable relationship; buying a large house in a good neighborhood; owning new cars; having nice children; becoming an officer in the firm or starting our own company; making lots of money; putting our children in "good" schools beginning with preschool; traveling to the "right" places; making the "right" connections; joining the proper clubs or groups; and being accepted into society. Through all of this it is implied that we should be happy. All the time. And we should be confident and proud, always looking to the future and the next goal that we can realize. And when we finally get to the last goal, our retirement, we will fall off the model (because it is only concerned with work and what we do) and possibly right out of life. What is wrong with this Doing model?

Advantages and Disadvantages

Nothing is wrong with the Doing model *if* it is recognized as severely limited and only used as a guide for a small portion of our lives. It is a relevant model for demonstrating status in middle- and upper-class America. It is clearly understood and reinforced in this society and it clearly defines how to belong and fit in. Also it is somewhat representative of the career path and may help some of us to structure what we want to do with the work part of our lives. It is known and familiar and therefore comfortable. Because many of us are dealing with the problems caused by the model, we are able to relate to others around us who share the same difficulties. It does teach us what we need to know and what we have to do in order to be defined as successful in society. We are acceptable to others as long as we stay on the course prescribed by this model. If we choose to stray from it, we become instant outsiders, rebels, deviants, or even pariahs. Therefore it becomes an easy way of distinguishing and discriminating—we are either on it or off it. If we are on, we belong, and if we are off, we do not.

Everything is wrong with this linear model when it is used as a guide for the whole of our lives. Remember, it is primarily concerned with achievement, and therefore the concept of being does not have relevance. This model defines us as "You are what you do," and society strongly reinforces this concept. Doing means working, which is defined as being productive, achieving, and having status. On the other hand not doing, not working, means being unproductive, lazy, unsuccessful, and is to be avoided at all times. There are many important things missing from this Western model if it is used, as it usually is, as the model for living. To begin with, the concept of Being, which is rather an abstract one, is simply not taught, included, or even considered. Other concepts, such as balance, wholeness, fate, luck, faith, spirituality, timing, self-discovery, alternate choices, alternative lifestyles, creativity, and emotional health, are either nonexistent or poorly represented on this goal-oriented linear model as well. When we step off the model by stopping, changing, or going "backward," we will find very little understanding or empathy from those still on it. We may experience anomie, the feeling that we are different and no longer belong. This alone will tell us that this linear model is not a flexible one.

The Danger

How can an entire society (and soon maybe the entire world as more and more countries emulate the Doing model) function using an inflexible, unidirectional model that is only concerned with achievement through work? The answer is very simple. It cannot. That fact is evident to all of those who have fallen or been pushed off the model and to those who work with physical, mental, and emotional health. This Western model is one that produces high stress. It is a model of nearly impossible expectations and some dangerous illusions. It may be an adequate model for some aspects of work and education, but it is dangerously inadequate for defining our whole selves and our entire lives.

Most of us have learned to define ourselves by what we do. When asked who we are, we usually answer by stating our profession. If we have a degree and a respectable (as defined by the model) profession, we feel proud to define ourselves by our work or position. If we do not, we may feel embarrassed or defensive and try to justify our lack of success. Also we tend to define ourselves by the outcome of our endeavors. For example being a writer is only impressive when we have been published; being a lawyer or teacher or doctor are only considered worthwhile occupations when we have substantial salaries. Thus success is determined by the end result and not by the endeavor or the individual's effort. Not having earning power translates into not being successful. The Western model implicitly teaches us that we must have a job *and* earn well in order to be considered successful. If earning a lot of money is not our goal, then we are often considered eccentric or even stupid. And to compound the situation, our worth in the world is determined, to a large extent, by how useful we are to others. Many of our social contacts may involve some degree of networking or being professionally viable. It is no surprise, then, that work subsumes our lives and becomes our primary focus for living. Most of us are taught to use our work to define ourselves, to describe our success, to belong, to have a sense of achievement, and ultimately to justify our value in the world.

The Reality

Work is really only what we do for eight hours a day, five days a week, more or less. Work is an activity and not a state of being. Work is a means to an end and never the end. Work is *not* all of life or even half of life. Our jobs are *not* who we are. It is a wonderful thing to have a job that we like much of the time, and to enjoy what we are doing and to do it well. All of these things can add a great deal of fulfillment to our lives. They can add to our lives, but never substitute for them. No matter what our jobs are, someone else can do them. No matter how powerful we are, someone else can take over. No matter how much status we think that we get from our work, the reality is that status, like an expensive suit, comes off when we are alone.

There is one positive thing about recognizing this model as absurd—the model then can take the blame for what we may have thought was our own failure or weakness or difficulty when we were trying to confuse doing with being and work with living. It is important to remember that most of us have not even recognized that this model exists; most of us have just been following what we have seen and known and been told to do. We are good students of a bad, or incomplete, model. It is not our fault that the goals delineated to us as worthwhile will not lead to the expected outcomes. We have all struggled to make sense of our lives, to do it "right," to be successful. We cannot be blamed for going down the wrong path when we were not aware that there was any other path to follow. The American Dream is powerful and pervasive—everyone who has heard of it wants a piece of it. All of this is natural. The myth it perpetuates is not often discovered until it is too late. We may recognize that very few of those around us, even those who are defined as successful, are really happy or balanced, but we will usually attribute this to some personal factor. Very few of us recognize that it is not the individual who fails but the model that is failing. The very few balanced and whole individuals who do exist will teach us that they have learned things that are not on this model. Just as we cannot learn arithmetic from reading a novel, so also we cannot learn internal worth, balance, wholeness, and inner peace from a model that only deals with externals. The simple fact that the Doing model is not appropriate for achieving true meaning in life is evident when we look around us and objectively observe what is happening to those following this model.

Childhood and Education

There are many casualties of this faulty model; the following are just a few of the more dramatic ones. Let us begin by observing our children. We do not have to look at the poor, deprived, or disabled ones (the model teaches us to ignore them), but instead focus on the crème de la crème—our bright, affluent, and gifted ones. Are they, as a whole, happy children? They have it all, or at least what society and their parents think is essential—good schools, competent teachers, nice homes, an extensive wardrobe, extracurricular activities, plenty of stimulation, expensive vacations, and so forth. Are these children balanced? Are they fun to be with? Do they enjoy their lives and are they enjoyable to be around? Are they disciplined? For far too many of these children it is a great sadness that the answer to these questions is *no*. These children, as a whole, are suffering. Many of them are superstressed and feel incredible pressure to achieve and succeed. Too many have already developed facades, meaning that they initially present themselves well. They may appear to be healthy and mature, but the facade easily cracks given the slightest stress or denial of their wants. They are the children of the model, and their education has been even more intense than ours was; they may be trained too well to be work and goal oriented. Certainly many are trying to be adults before they have been children. Frequently they are required to make decisions they are not capable of making and they are expected to experience life from an adult perspective. Hence they become pseudoadults or overly sophisticated children. It is important for parents to recognize that the child's "work" is to play and to learn and that the child's needs are to be loved and structured. Children are masters at "being" and can teach adults the value of playing and being in this world. Unfortunately, instead of learning how to be from them, our society has forced them onto the Doing model.

When we look at society's conception of education, we will see another symptom of the model. This concept values education as the means to a "good" job (high paying, high status), rather than being educated as a goal unto itself. In the past the concept of education meant becoming well rounded, well read, literate, and knowledgeable about a variety of subjects. Then there was a clear distinction between being educated (the university) and being trained (technical schools). The latter prepared one for a job and developed the skills necessary to work. The university provided the classical concept of education and was not expected to provide specific skills or work-related training. This distinction no longer exists in this country. The proliferation of business schools and technical schools within universities, the emphasis on career training, the general lack of interest for the classical education, and the overriding concern for college training as the means to a career attest to the change in defining education. The emphasis on skilled training and the importance of being educated in order to achieve work-related goals begins early in our culture. Many young children are already concerned about their future careers while they are still in primary school. Our society places too much pressure on children to achieve (make good grades) and rarely rewards the idea of learning for its own sake. Thus very young children, who are naturally balanced when allowed to be, are forced into competing, winning, achieving at any price, and becoming un-balanced. The cost of adherence to the Western model is very high—we are losing our children and they are losing their childhoods.

Adolescence

The next casualty is our adolescents. We might think that the model would love teenagers, as they are major consumers of material goods. But if we look at this model closely, we will see that there is hardly any time allotted to this decade in life. The only thing a teenager can do on the Western model is to learn skills that will lead to a job. Thus the adolescent needs to (a) go to school—this is a must in order to remain on the model; (b) make good grades; and (c) get into a "good" col-lege. If the adolescent cannot make it at this level, he (or she) will have no chance for future success, as defined by the model and society. The Doing model has not changed since its incep-tion, but present economic conditions can no longer deliver what this model promises. Some relevant facts of life in Amer-ica today are the following: (a) there are not enough good schools; (b) some of us were not created to be good students; and (c) higher education was not designed for everyone and never should have become a universal goal.

For many adolescents the model really becomes ugly when they are faced with life decisions. If they are not securely on the model by their early twenties, it is almost impossible to get back onto it. These adolescents can never again compete with those who have stayed on the model. This is not only dangerous, but discriminatory and even evil. There are too many adolescents who have been forced away from the life they would like to have simply because the model for this life is extremely limited and prejudicial. To give up on a desired life, be realistically depressed, see choices disappear before the end of the second decade of life is an unbelievably bleak prospect for the future. Yet this happens to an increasing number of teenagers each year. And unless this becomes a political issue or a fashionable crusade, society—as reflected by the model—does not and will not care too much for these underprivileged adolescents who cannot "make it."

Young Adults

Next let us follow the individuals in their twenties who have stayed on the model. So far they have followed all the implicit rules: They have obtained good educations, made good grades, been good students and citizens, and are now ready for that first good job. But where is it? Society has trained us to expect that when we do all the "right" things and work diligently, we will succeed. It has defined success as having the "right" kind of job paying a good salary. One of the realities of the nineties is that these "good" jobs are rare, and there are no indications of economic changes in the foreseeable future. For those in their twenties who are facing this dilemma, there seem to be limited options. If they do not get a good job, then they cannot stay on the model, head up the corporate ladder, and make that first million by the time they are forty. There is no answer for this dilemma on the Doing model. It is no wonder that so many young adults in this society feel as if they are failures and that they have been cheated. Many of them feel desperate to get out and be a success and they are very frustrated that they cannot do so. Too many of them are dissatisfied with their work and their lives and depressed by their situations.

Adulthood

One final example should suffice to demonstrate how insidious and dangerous this model is. Let us observe those who are in their forties or fifties and have done everything according to plan. They may be managers in their organizations, they may have moved several times to progressively better positions and neighborhoods, they belong to the right clubs and are saving money to put their children into the best universities. Now the organization has decided to downgrade, and this enterprising and mature adult is one of the many casualties. This is currently happening to thousands of previously successful managerial types, who are being thrown off the model through no fault of their own. As with the twenty-year-olds, there does not seem to be much hope in the future. Current economic conditions make it difficult to replace a lost job with a similar new one. What are they going to do? And if they are now off the model, what will happen to their children? How are they going to be able to get the education they need? The tragedy of following the Doing model, giving all to one's job, is that once the job is gone, there is nothing else left. This situation affects not only the dismissed employee but also the spouse and family, who have probably based their status and worth on the externals produced by the job. An entire family faces the prospect of being thrown off the model and losing its position in society. It really is not right, and it is not fair, but this model does not care. And the prevailing attitude in society is generally "Glad it's not me."

The Reality of the Doing Model

All of the foregoing demonstrates that this model is incredibly incomplete. There is no recognition of fate or timing. There is no acknowledgment of luck. Sometimes we may get things, including jobs, simply because we are lucky, or in the right place at exactly the right time, or due to circumstances that are not in our control. And sometimes we do not get the things we deserve because we are unlucky or the timing is bad. All the hard work, best intentions, and positive expectations in the world cannot guarantee our successes. There will always be things that are out of our control; fate, luck, timing, and outside variables are always operating. The most important thing to learn is never to confuse our work with our *Selves* and never to blame ourselves for things that we cannot be completely responsible for, such as getting the right job or being financially lucky. Whenever the situation is out of our control and we are not getting what we want, we need to be creative and flexible; unfortunately the model has not trained us to do so and society does not usually reward these qualities. The Doing model has not taught us to look for other choices along the way. It has not trained us to be well rounded and balanced; it has not taught us to be creative so that if one thing does not work, we can try another. Many of us have been trained in this age of specificity and have difficulties generalizing our training.

The Doing model has not taught us to be empathetic toward others, but rather to view them as competitors and vie against them for what we achieve. This model is based on the "win-lose" concept and therefore teaches us to be competitive, judgmental, and to win at the expense of others. Winning is the ultimate goal. Thus the model is restrictive, inflexible, limited, and ultimately inhumane. It is no wonder, then, that so many of us have come to demonstrate these same qualities. This model is a guide to affluence and therefore not representative of, or followed by, the entire population. It is, however, the representative map of the American Dream. It is the ideal that best represents what immigrants hope for when they arrive in this country. Finally, it is the goal that the world now seems to aspire to, as more countries give up their traditional beliefs and cultures in order to emulate Western ways. It is a powerful force because so many people give it power. It is the dominant model for setting goals and realizing dreams and it has become a way of life for millions of people. It is also used to define and set the standard of success. Few have questioned it, and society at large has never really challenged it, even though it is a model that just does not work!

What Is Taught

Let us suppose that we are among the relatively few "lucky" ones who have stayed on the model throughout our lives and have thus been defined (by its standards) as productive and successful. Let us take a hard look at some of the things we have learned, overtly or implicitly, from this model of success. This model, as previously stated, applies to a limited few; there simply are not enough economic or status rewards, considered essential for success, to satisfy everyone. Therefore most of us have learned to do anything we can in order to succeed. We will compete with anyone to get what we want, because winning has become one of the most important activities in our lives. As a result we have learned to value power and control over others and to work hard to win while someone else loses.

Respectability is also very important, and we have learned always to look "right." Our facades are usually well developed and our status in the world, as mentioned before, comes from our achievements, which have been defined by this model. Most of these accomplishments require comparisons with others in order to be meaningful. Thus we have become masters at comparing and judging others. We have probably spent a lot of time looking at ourselves in relation to those around us. This model requires that we have others to look down on in order to feel worthy and successful and to help measure our achievements. Those beneath or behind us tell us how far we have come. It also requires some others to look up to as a measure of our future dreams, aspirations, and goals. Those ahead of us tell us how far we still have to go. We need to be impressive to some and to be impressed by others, all of which means continually making judgments. Because of this competitive, critical nature the Doing model focuses on the negative aspects of others. It thrives on finding differences. An important paradox exists here: We originally wanted to be on the model in order to find belonging and closeness with others, but the longer we are on it, the more differences we seek and the more alienated we become.

The Myth of Perfection

We can easily see how this is a model of stress. The amount of pressure generated from trying to follow this path of success is incredibly high. Being on the model creates pressure because we can *never stop*. There are no rest areas along the way. Someone else is always right behind us trying to take our place or pass us by. Someone is always right in front of us showing us what must still be accomplished. The one sure thing we realize in order to survive on this model is that we must try to be perfect. The illusion that perfectionism is attainable is dangerous; yet we are a nation that rewards its perfectionists and punishes its imperfect ones. Many of us will have difficulty believing that perfection is an illusion because it is so ingrained in our culture. We want to do perfect jobs, present perfect ideas, have perfect relationships, and rear perfect children. We want our homes, vacations, jobs, and appearances to be perfect. Many of us continue to work toward this perfect state, which does not exist. The resistance to accepting the myth of perfection is very high because the illusion is powerful and pervasive—we really do want to be perfect, to do things perfectly, and to have perfect lives.

If we have any doubts about how consumed we are with this concept of perfection, all we have to do is observe ourselves and question others around us. Ask any teacher about the phenomenon of the student who makes an "A" on an exam but is miserable because he did not make an "A-plus." Ask attractive people what they do not like about their appearance. Ask those who are perceived as successful how they are feeling about their lives. Congratulate someone on doing a good job. Pay compliments to others. In most instances we will quickly see from the responses given that people in general are trying to be perfect and are not able to accept or be content with themselves, even when they are doing well. We are simply not taught how to be positive, satisfied, or to say "enough." We are trained to want more, do more, try to be perfect, or at the very least appear so to others. How can we be perfect? Humans are not designed to attain perfection. Why would anyone want to set a goal that is against his own nature, the antithesis of his very being? Perhaps the answer is that the Western model implies that the only way for us to be happy and secure is to strive for perfection in all things. This is crazy-making!

If we have any further doubts about being competitive, striving for perfection, needing status by external validation, or fearing failure and the taking of personal responsibility, all we have to do is look at and listen to what is valued, bragged about, and taught. We might begin with the popular bumper sticker on many parents' cars: *My Child Is an Honor Roll Student at Western Model Elementary.* It would be refreshing and encouraging to see a bumper sticker that said, *I Am the Proud Parent of a Well-Balanced, Wonderful Child Who Has Never Made an Honor Roll.* Next we can question the ideas behind the bumper stickers that say, *American, Love It or Leave It* and *Don't Blame Me, I Voted for the Other Guy.* How encouraging it would be to see one that said, *The Buck Stops Here* or *I Will Take Some Responsibility for This Mess* or even *I Admit Something's Wrong and Am Willing to Work on It!*

Next we can look at our automobiles and what they represent. A friend of mine, looking at my daughter's 1969 VW Beetle, said, "When we come right down to it, that's all we really need for transportation." He was right. Much of the time we buy cars to represent our status, success, competition with others, and to provide external satisfaction for our achievement. This is also demonstrated by our houses, jewelry, and clothes when we are more concerned with impressing others than satisfying ourselves. In fact what we really need is relatively minimal. What we are trained to want is usually involved with making an impression, feeling important, and looking successful. We are taught to envy and to make others envious. In reality these are not the goals that do much for the internal person, the soul, or the spirit.

The Facade of Success

The effects of our achievement-oriented training are everywhere. If we go into any bookstore and look at the best-sellers, we will find that there are many more books about how to win, how to be successful and powerful, how to impress others or get what we want through others than there are about dealing with our internal selves and becoming whole and balanced. (Fortunately for society there are now best-sellers that deal with these topics: *The Road Less Traveled, Care of the Soul, The Celestine Prophecy,* and *The Seven Spiritual Laws of Success,* to name a few.) There are many more how-to-succeed books dealing with business, finance, marriage, relationships, and health. For every book that discusses the internal self, the spirit, or the soul, there must be hundreds that deal with the externals. We can easily find books that tell us how to improve our looks, dress for success, act sexy, or shape and reshape our bodies. This obsession with our physical appearance is also attributable to the Western model. It is not enough to be successful, we must also look successful. That is usually defined as looking young, tanned, energetic, slim, happy, and well dressed. It often means appearing to be healthy, which can be quite different from actually being healthy. Also we can see the effects of the model when we stay at home and pick up a magazine or turn on the television. If we focus only on commercials and advertisements, we will quickly learn that the critical measure of worth in this culture is to look successful. Almost all advertising is geared to appearance, status, and external attributes. The internal self and the development of true life meaning are rarely, if ever, dealt with or deemed effective by advertisers for selling a product.

The Power Illusion

We have also been taught that power and control are necessary components of success and worth. We are not taught that they are two of our biggest illusions. We are not trained to realize that we can only have power over someone else when they, overtly or covertly, give us that power. The moment that they stop giving it is the moment we lose it. Power is not something we can own or have or carry around or keep. It is not something that is ours; power always belongs to the givers and never the takers. If we have difficulty with the concept that power needs the powerless in order to exist, all we have to consider are our power systems. In all these systems, whether it be the military, prisons, schools, or any other institution, or any type of hierarchy, including organizations, religions, and social and political groups, power is a function of those who are perceived as powerless allowing those who are perceived as powerful to exist. When the weak ones successfully revolt (a rare phenomenon) and, by sheer numbers or force, reclaim or assert the power they have previously given away, the power system disappears or drastically changes. Perhaps that is why "power struggles" are frequently encountered in our lives.

If we think about the people we have power over and then consider what happens when they disagree with us, we will quickly perceive that power is a nebulous concept. We may want to question the security of our own power base. Imagine for a moment that everyone over whom we have power gets together and decides to go against our wishes. We may indeed have some way of averting this revolt, but where does our power come from? Is it externally (position, authority) or internally (charisma, expertise) determined? Meanwhile what is happening to our feelings of power? Is this what we were trained to expect? If we are now feeling confused or powerless, we can blame it on our training. It is not our fault that we learned to have an illusion of power; remember, we have been good students of a bad model.

Power Versus Control

Having control is generally perceived as synonymous with having power, but what we can and cannot control are somewhat different from those over whom we exert power. Researchers of organizational management have defined power according to types: referent power (charisma), expert power (perception of knowledge or expertise), coercive power (force or fear), legitimate power (authority), reward power (the ability to reinforce), information power and connection power (link to someone with power). All power except internal power (the power derived from loving the Self) has one thing in common: it depends upon others in order to exist. The Western model requires that power be "real" in order for the concept to be meaningful. The fact that the subordinate gives power to the dominant one (and therefore holds the true power) is rarely emphasized. When we are given power, someone else is doing the giving and can decide to stop. Thus, perceiving ourselves as powerful because of external sources is an illusion.

With respect to others, power and control are very much alike. We can control those who, for whatever reason, allow us to control them. (There are obvious exceptions to this: small children, animals, the helpless and the handicapped, anyone who literally cannot survive without the help of others. Rather than allowing us to control them, these exceptions may require being controlled in order to survive.) We can control those who benefit from being controlled. However, at any time those being controlled may leave, or grow up, or tire of the role of dependent, and we may find them trying to control us. All of this sounds remarkably like the discussion about power. What, then, is the difference between the two?

The Reality of Control

There are two, and *only* two, things in the world that we can absolutely control, now and forever. This is because these two things require only ourselves and have nothing to do with anyone else.

First, we can control the way we feel about ourselves. This can be defined as our choices to like or not like ourselves, to love or hate ourselves, to feel positively or negatively toward ourselves, or to ignore ourselves entirely. No one else can make this choice for us, and we cannot choose for someone else, which is why our self-esteem is totally within our control.

Second, we can control our own behavior based on our feelings. We can choose what we are going to do. We can start and stop our chosen behavior at any time. We can act or react in the manner that we want whenever we want. No one else can behave for us, and even though we may want to or even try to do so, we cannot behave for anyone else. Therefore we have complete control over our behavior based on our feelings.

It is important to note that controlling the way we feel about ourselves does not mean that we can control our feelings. We cannot. Our feelings may be ours, but they are not in our control. When we remember the times that others tried to hurt us, or to blame us unfairly, or to do injury to our possessions, we will also remember that we had strong feelings about these situations. We could no more control what we were feeling at these times than we could control what was happening to us. We could not stop feeling upset just because we wanted to feel better.

The way we feel about ourselves is a conscious and deliberate process and it requires a choice. We may have been trained to feel good about ourselves when everything is fine and to feel bad about ourselves when everything is a mess. If so, we are among the many who have been misled by our training. If we believe that we have to perform well in order to be "good" and that making mistakes and being imperfect are "bad," then we must also believe that we can always control the consequences of our actions. We have also probably been taught to confuse power and control with responsibility. The model implicitly teaches us that we are responsible for things when they go wrong or do not work, and therefore we should feel bad about ourselves when bad things occur.

Conversely the model teaches us that when things go well and work out, there are other factors present to account for this success, so we cannot feel *too* good about ourselves. Remember, this is a self-defeating model. The secret about control is that we cannot be completely responsible for that which we cannot control (with the same exceptions noted above). If we can control it, we are responsible for it. Then it becomes very clear that we are responsible for the way we feel about ourselves. We make the choices—we choose to feel good or bad, loved or hated—and we act on these choices.

Controlling Behavior

We can control our feelings about ourselves and we can also control our behavior based on these feelings. Again, this concept does not mean that we can control *all* our behavior. There are many physical actions that are unconscious to us and therefore not in our control. When we are asleep and our body moves, we cannot control such movements. We cannot control our digestive system, our circulatory system, our sympathetic and parasympathetic systems (at least not completely and not very well). Therefore the qualification of controlling behavior based on our feelings becomes important. Once again, the critical issue here is one of choice. No matter what we are feeling, we can choose how we will behave. Our training may have led us to believe that certain actions are determined by our feelings: When we are sad, we cry; when we are angry, we yell; when we are afraid, we shake. In reality we choose what we will do based on what we feel, and hopefully we will not always choose the same behavior. Each of us has the potential for a large repertoire of behavior; each of us can choose and therefore control what we will do. Nobody else can make us behave in a certain manner unless we allow him to do so, and thereby give him the illusion of control over us.

Resolving the Problem

Once we recognize that our training about power and control is faulty and learn that these concepts are really just illusions, then we can begin to concentrate on the realities of power and control. Hopefully we can also extend this recognition to our illusion of work as our main reason for life. We can now begin to focus on the totality of our lives, in which work is only one component, though not necessarily the critical one. Work is a reality of life; no one can expect to dispense with it, nor would we want to. In and of itself work is not the reason for most of our problems. The difficulty is not work itself, but rather the expectations and illusions we have attributed to it. When work is no longer confused with life, when doing is not regarded as more important than being, when success is not defined by externals, and when we are not focused solely on achieving in order to impress others, then we are still in the real world, but we are off the Doing model. And most of our problems concerning work will have disappeared or become manageable.

The Being Model

It may be helpful to present another model at this time: the Eastern model, so named because it is representative of the types of training based on Oriental or Eastern religions, philosophies, and cultures. Just as the Western one is presented as the *Doing* model, the Eastern one can be conceived of as the *Being* model. In contrast with the linear Doing model, the Being model can be represented by a circle spiraling inward with no clear beginning and no known end. Thus we can begin to use the Being model anytime we desire; in contrast to the Doing model, we do not have to *do* anything in order to *be*. There is no better or best place to be on the Being model, as all places are equal. The focus is simply upon the Self. We are not concerned with where others are or their relevance to us, so there is no competition with them or judgment of them. Our goals have been realized the moment we adopted this model; simply being on it is the only goal. This model probably has only one clear expectation, and it is that we will learn. No matter what else may happen, we will learn. We may never arrive at a destination, because we cannot know the end results of living. The spiral is a representation of the journey of life, and as such it is about process. The Being model is an objective one; learning is the only achievement, and the only task may be to resolve the opposites, find the similarities, and discover the interrelationship among all things. By using this model we no longer need to dichotomize: Nothing needs to be labeled good or bad, right or wrong, success or failure, perfect or imperfect. The premise is very simple: *Being* means becoming actively aware of our being—our Selves, our internal environment, and eventually our connections to all.

Those who have discovered the Being model love it and love themselves when they are on it. Paradoxically they also more easily love others and actually exhibit more loving behavior than those on the Doing model, which tends to emphasize getting love more than giving it. The wonderful thing about the Eastern model is that we can incorporate the Western one into it; we can stop using the Doing model as our only framework for life and living. Thus we can set work-related goals, value our education, and sometimes choose to move linearly, but we can also move beyond doing and choose to focus on being. The spiral teaches us to focus on loving ourselves and satisfying our own needs at whatever point in time we exist. It allows us to accept the reality of ourselves in this moment. It does not teach us to achieve external goals or to acquire possessions; instead it allows us to practice Being and stop Doing all the time. It reinforces relaxing, slowing down, and taking it easy. Life does not have to be hard all the time. There is balance and harmony, sense and reason, beauty and joy all around us at all times. Living on the Doing model is living on the edge (after all, it is a linear model). It is like wearing blinders and seeing only a fraction of the world. The Being model allows us to expand our vision; it allows us to recognize the circularity of life. We can take the blinders off. We can really live! We can learn to be!

The best way to adopt and use the Being model is to begin by learning acceptance. Working through the seven problem-solving steps will not only help resolve difficulties with work issues, it will also teach us the art of Being.

Being and Doing

The Being model does not imply that we should not do any-thing at all; it does not mean that we should withdraw from the world and meditate atop some remote mountain. Very few would choose such an extreme lifestyle. Rather, Being is about accepting all facets of ourselves and our lives, becoming bal-anced and harmonious, secure and safe for ourselves. Conse-quently Doing will become a necessary and positive part of Being. This usually means working in some capacity in order to be self-productive and somewhat self-sufficient. All of us have strong yearnings to do something well, to accomplish personal goals, and to feel creative and positive about ourselves. Unfor-tunately the Doing model reinforces extrinsic goals for work—those things outside of ourselves. We need to refocus and learn to work for intrinsic rewards, those internal things that make each of us happy. An important part of Being concerns learning to acknowledge and honor our creative sides, becoming self-motivated and self-satisfied, and developing a personal sense of accomplishment. Being leads to contentment, peace of mind, self-worth, and the recognition of when we are doing our best no matter what the results. Work, then, can become a creative, fulfilling, and important source of our life satisfaction; this can only occur when we are driven by our own needs and internal desires. When these become our primary motivations for work, we tend to love what we do and to do it because we want to, not because we have to. When work is defined as "love made visible," we are actually demonstrating the love we have for ourselves and the respect and worth for what we are doing. Being and Doing become interrelated when we feel loving toward ourselves, positive about our actions, and can recognize the connection between the two. Our worth is not determined by our work, but our work often reflects how we perceive our worth. Likewise, Doing is part of Being, and it reflects how we perceive ourselves. The concept of Being, however, involves much more than just Doing. It is the integration of all parts of our whole, it is everything we are, have been, and will be and it involves our connections to others and to God. It is much more comprehensive than anything we have been taught to work toward. In short we are not Being in order to Do, which leads to imbalance; instead we are Doing and not Doing in order to Be. This awareness will lead to balance and harmony.

II ∽ Problem-Solving Work

1. Accepting

Begin your problem-solving process by accepting the fact that your training about the relationship between life and work has probably been faulty and incomplete. This is a hard one! If you can accept this, you will be able to recognize that you are not completely responsible for your successes, much as you may wish to be, nor are you totally responsible for your failures, although you may have gotten used to taking the blame for them. You will also recognize that you control very little, that external power is an illusion, perfection is unattainable, and your worth is not determined by external possessions. Accepting all this means that you will begin to develop a whole new way of thinking, talking, and attributing cause. But before you begin trying to change or solve your problems, spend some time thinking and accepting. This is always the hardest part of the process—letting things be just the way they are and looking at them as objectively as possible. This is what acceptance means; it does not mean that you are agreeing with or condoning but that you are objectively viewing. More simply, it means that you are facing the reality of yourself, your situation, and your difficulties.

The Doing model has taught you to have unrealistic expectations about work and success. It has trained you how to define yourself to the world (through externals and others) and that you must compete, judge, and never stop doing. You have learned that winning is more important than anything, appearance is more important than reality, and that you can never work too hard, be too rich, or have too much success. This model can be dangerous, and faithfully following it will probably kill you—if not physically, then emotionally and spiritually. Accept this. Also accept the fact that you are more than your training, more than what others perceive, and that your life is more than work or what you do. The Doing model cannot get you where you really want to go. Although the Being model is not focused on movement, paradoxically it is the model that will cause you to move. Learn to accept that life is paradox. Recognize that all this acceptance is difficult and often feels awkward and strange; this is because it is an unfamiliar process. Finally, accept that others may not understand your new perceptions and that society will not reward your awareness of the faults in its favorite model. But that is acceptable because you will experience what it is like to *be;* you will no longer always need external approval or esteem from others. You will know where the meaningful approval is—inside yourself.

II · *Problem-Solving Work* ☜ 35

2. Letting Go

All this acceptance is difficult, but it is critical in order to begin the next step. Here you will need to let go of your framework of life, move past your previous training, confront the realities, release the illusions, and learn new concepts about the meaning of life. Society through the Doing model has structured much of your life and the lives of those around you. How can you begin to let go of what you know? The answer is: slowly. Let go slowly. Begin by letting go of Doing as the foundation of your entire life and limit it to your work life. In this way you can keep your familiar goals but begin to expand your vision and broaden your perceptions. It is always easier to add to something than it is to subtract from it. Add the concept of Being to your life. This requires you to let go of some of your old expectations and illusions about work. Let go of the notion that what you do determines who you are. You are much more than what you do. Anyone who has ever cared for you knows that. Let go of the idea that you always have to know what you want or need. The model has taught you that you have to be confident and sure, assertive and strong. Let go of all that. In the privacy of yourself, let go of your facade and allow yourself to be confused and unsure. Feel a little weak. This defeats your weak ego, the need for esteem from others, which keeps you living in your facade, always appearing strong and in control and seeing yourself only through the perceptions of others. Being vulnerable and fragile at times helps to keep the weak ego down to a manageable size. You will never get rid of it, but you can prevent it from dominating your life and making you miserable.

Let go of being so competitive. When you do, you will find it easier to stop always judging others. Ouch!! This one sounds really difficult. When you begin to let go of your needs to be perfect, to be right, to be strong, to be powerful, and always to be in control, you will discover that letting go of the need to judge and compete with others will become quite easy. Learn a secret here: You judge others when you feel insecure about yourself. You criticize others in order to feel better about yourself or to justify and excuse your own behavior. Thus you judge others most often when you are feeling negative toward yourself. Therefore the easiest way to stop judging is to start being positive about yourself.

Let go of your crazy training—you do not have to compare yourself to anyone else. You are you, you are good, and everything you do is part of your unique journey, part of your being. Let go of the idea that you have to explain everything. Admit that sometimes you do not know and tell yourself that is okay. Let go of the idea that all your successes and failures were in your control. Let go of the idea that you are really powerful, unless you are recognizing your self-power. Let go of what you have been taught about control. If you focus on controlling only that which is truly in your control, you will be dealing only with yourself. Forget trying to control the world, the future, or anyone else.

When all this letting go is finished, you will certainly feel much lighter. When you let go of power and control, you also let go of responsibility. That feels great. When you let go of competition and judgment, you also let go of the concept of perfection. That feels right. And when you let go of the idea that work is life, you immediately expand your boundaries, open to new possibilities, and begin to change and actually feel yourself grow. And that feels wonderful!

3. Expressing Feelings

As you were trying to do the accepting and letting go exercises, you were probably aware of all kinds of feelings. You surely felt anger at some type of betrayal. After all, you did not invent the model, and surely someone else older than you, such as your parents, discovered that it was faulty and incomplete. Why did they train you on this model? Why didn't they teach you about other things, such as balance and wholeness and fulfilling your own needs? How dare they perpetuate their own illusions upon you? So of course you are going to be angry, if not at your parents, then at society. Express your anger. Get it out so that you can get going. Yell and scream and rage at the injustice of it all. You are right. It is not fair, it is not right, it is not just. Be angry, but do not take your anger out on anyone else. Remember, they also were trained on the same model, and what has happened to you is not their, or anyone else's, fault. Also, you are most likely feeling hurt. How could you, smart and skilled as you are, not have figured it out by now? And if you did, why didn't you know what to do? These feelings are all natural residual effects of becoming disillusioned. Get them out and go on.

You are right: Your faulty training is a scam. You have been conned. Government, society, institutions, organizations, social units, and even your family systems do not exist to make you all right. They exist to further themselves and to do what works to maintain the status quo. You are a cog, a tiny part, a fraction of the whole picture—if you think in terms of the Western model. If you look at the Eastern one, however, you are all that matters. At times you need to focus on one and at other times, the other. The Eastern model will teach you how to take care of your own needs, desires, and how to be. The Western one will teach you how to communicate and how to belong in this society, and it will help you to understand some of the craziness out there. You may feel confused about how to use these models. Express these feelings, but do not let them stop you from practicing Being. You will soon find that expanding your model and placing the Doing model within the larger Being model becomes natural and easy. You will use the Doing model for a very limited part of your life and you will want to spend more and more time Being.

Please remember that you cannot control your feelings but that you can control your behaviors. Express your feelings, if only to yourself. No one else needs to know what you are feeling every time you feel something; you yourself, however, must be aware and recognize your feelings, if only for the briefest moment, in order to let them out. Expressing or acknowledging your own feelings stops them from accumulating inside you. Expressing your feelings allows you to know that you are alive, you are real, and you are human. Doing so allows you to become aware of what changes you will need to make in yourself and in your life in accordance with your feelings. You are a feeling being, and that may well be your most significant accomplishment as a living being. Without problems you would have little reason to feel. Feeling and being are often synonymous. Feeling and doing are not, as doing often requires either acting upon, negating, or denying your emotions. Feelings do not require any of these responses; they only require acknowledgment. Practice feeling; practice being.

4. Taking Responsibility

It is very difficult to take responsibility for your training on a model that you had nothing to do with creating. So please do not try to be responsible for your faulty learning. But as soon as you recognize that your training has been incomplete and that following the Western model will not help you achieve your personal goals or desires, you become responsible for your choices. You will be especially responsible for perpetuating this model upon your children or those under you who are vulnerable and unaware. You are now responsible, because you now know, that the Doing model is not going to work for all areas of your life or your children's lives. This responsibility means that you need either to seek an alternative, to lower your expectations, or to try to fight the system. You can try to force the model to work or you can waste your time trying to change society. These are all possible choices, and you are responsible if you choose self-defeating behaviors and self-destructive options. Nobody else will be responsible for your choices. Actually only a very few will realize or care that you are expanding your choices and discovering another way of being. Possibly some of those who observe your change will become frightened or threatened. However, you cannot give up your own quest in order to appease others or to stop them from being afraid. You can only do what you must for your own life. Not everyone will understand or approve, but they are not responsible for you. Only you can be responsible for your Self, your life, your choices, and your well-being. You are also responsible for being a good role model for your children.

5. Forgiving

You can only forgive those who have responsibility for what is being forgiven. In order to have responsibility, they must have control. If they are not responsible—not in control—then they cannot be forgiven, because forgiveness first implies blame. Whom are you going to blame for your being on the Doing model? What or who is responsible for your faulty training? How are you going to forgive society for being wrong, for perpetuating myths and illusions and expectations that lead to disappointments, depressions, and sometimes disasters? Yes, you can hold society responsible for many of your problems, but what good does that actually do you as an individual? You can certainly express your anger at society. You can blame your ailments and confusion on society. You can try to change society or even try to leave it.

But until you begin with yourself, and not with what is out

there, you will only be wasting your own precious time. You can only forgive yourself for that part of the training for which you are personally responsible, and that will not be much. You can, however, forgive yourself for hesitating to learn a new way of being. You can forgive yourself for being afraid of losing some of the things you have been trained to believe are important. You can also forgive yourself for your innate needs to belong to your society, your culture, your organization, and your family, even if belonging demands too high a personal price. You can forgive yourself for your illusions, myths, and expectations that have kept you following the Doing model and are keeping you on it right now. You can forgive your unrealistic hopes and dreams, such as wanting to win the lottery or become famous or own the dream. You can forgive yourself for all of these things if, and only *if,* you do not let your forgiveness stop you from choosing to change, learn, grow, and discover other ways of being that are more productive and positive.

In other words you cannot forgive yourself for staying on the Doing model just because it is known and therefore familiar; you cannot forgive yourself for not taking a risk and practicing Being. You cannot forgive yourself for not taking the blame and responsibility for your own choices. You cannot forgive yourself as a means to give up, cop out, or delegate your life to the model. You cannot forgive yourself for something that you have not first blamed yourself for; second, taken responsibility for; and third, really wanted to change. Forgiveness is not an alternative to change or choice. It is not an "instead of" proposition. You cannot say, "I will forgive instead of dealing with the reality, letting go of the excuses, expressing my true feelings, and taking responsibility for my part." Only when you have done these things can you forgive. And when you truly forgive, you let go and move on.

6. Appreciating

This step may sound very simple, but in reality it is one of the more difficult ones, probably because you do it so rarely. How can you appreciate what you have learned from a model that has taught you so inappropriately? And what exactly is there to appreciate anyway? You are unhappy and confused and have unrealistic hopes and dreams; your values are materialistic and you have lost touch with your own feelings and desires; you pay way too much attention to what others think and hardly any to yourself. And now you are being told to appreciate all that. How can you?

You can begin by appreciating the fact that you are here; you have survived. This is no mean feat. Appreciate the fact that you want to change, or you would not be reading all this. Appreciate the fact that despite your adherence to the Western model, your humanity is still intact. Because this model is primarily about achievement, accumulation, and things outside of your Self, you can appreciate the fact that it has dealt very little with your spirit, soul, and inner self. By ignoring these things it has not done them irreparable harm. And above all appreciate your own unhappiness, confusion, and uncertainty. These miseries have brought you to the place and state of taking a risk, seeking a new path, finding other answers. These "negative" things have brought you to this "positive" place.

If you think and look hard enough, you will find things that you did and learned while on the Doing model that you can appreciate. It is a realistic model for some aspects of your life—it works for work. The model teaches you how to belong in this society and what you must do to achieve worldly success. True, it is incomplete, but you can appreciate that it is your starting place for questioning and discovering other options and choices. It has taught you that education is important, which is a truth that you can clearly appreciate. The model may be erroneous about why this is so—education is ideally not the means to an end but the end in itself—but any emphasis on education is good. The Doing model was your beginning; now you will want to continue on the Being model. It is always important to appreciate your beginnings. After all, they brought you here.

7. Rewarding

If you can jump off the Doing model for just a moment and imagine yourself on a model for life that has no demands, no criticisms, no judgments, no competition, no dichotomies, no pressure, and no stress, you may feel that you have died and gone to heaven. But you are still alive and here on earth and you need to know that people using the Being model do very well living in the reality of this world. This concept of Being has been around for a long time and is recognized and valued by all religions. The Eastern philosophies and religions embrace it as the core of their beliefs. Western religions aspire and allude to it as being "Christian" or in a "state of grace." The rewards for actively Being are legion. What you have not been taught is how to get there; the reason for this can be found in the Western way of thinking and talking about Being. This means using goal-oriented, achievement-directed language and process to try to "get" this state of Being, as if it exists outside of yourself. This training means that you do not know how to recognize and reward the value of nonachievement or lack of goals; you have not learned that what is important is the process itself, the journey rather than the end. This is what you must now do in order to *be*.

Reward yourself right now for where you are, who you are, what you are. Pat yourself on your back. Give yourself a treat. Do something you want to do. Do it because you are being. It is not vice versa, as we have been taught; this is not being because you are doing. Sometimes even reward yourself when you are doing absolutely nothing. Because in fact you really are not doing no thing—you are always being. At times reward yourself for nonmovement. Being still is one of the hardest things that you have not been taught to do. Reward yourself for an empty mind; enlightenment only occurs when the thoughts are still. Again you have never been taught the value of still, quiet nondoing. And these things are unbelievably difficult. Passively try not to feel. This is a very different process from actively ignoring or repressing your feelings. Reward yourself every time you are passively still and actively aware of your own stillness. You are truly Being.

Practicing Being is not easy. The goal here is unusual because it has already been achieved. You are Being. Whether you choose to practice it, ignore it, or try not to do it, you are still Being. You are never not Being. When you are Doing, you are Being first. The paradox is that you are always Being, but until you value and recognize the process, it will not have meaning for you. And once you value and recognize this state that is always there, the doing of it actually becomes quite difficult, at least in the beginning. Reward yourself for the recognition that Being is the only way to achieve your Self and that the awareness of Being is the important and difficult part of the process. Reward yourself for practicing something that is difficult to do and easy to ignore. Reward yourself for trying a skill that has not been in your training. The more you reward yourself, the more you are practicing the awareness of Being and the easier it will become for you to let go and let be. All of this is hard but very valuable and clearly deserving of self-rewards.

Money often costs too much.

—Ralph Waldo Emerson

III ∽ *Money*

If work provides the arena in which to achieve "success," as defined by the Western model, then money becomes the ultimate measure of having achieved it. In our culture success and money are so closely interrelated that when we speak of realizing the American dream, or "making it," the underlying assumption is that we have become wealthy. We are implicitly taught to believe that the easiest way to measure achievement and worth in the world is to count the amount of money we have. If we are rich, we have achieved success; if we are not rich, we have not. There is a well-known supposition that people who are wealthy enough can do almost anything and get away with it—including murder, tax evasion, corruption. They can buy whatever they want—including status, fame, love, and even other people. Perhaps that is why the possession of wealth is desired above the possession of morals, values, character, and education. The quest for wealth has become a type of religion; wanting money may even supersede wanting God. Certainly there are many adherents of the search-for-life-meaning through obtaining wealth; there are many who perceive this quest as the ultimate one of their lives. For them no amount of money can ever be enough; they truly believe that "there is no such thing as being too rich." For many of these monetary pilgrims, it is not just the money itself but what it can buy that becomes their driving force and defines their lives. These individuals tend to become obsessed with possessions and develop unlimited needs for external things, which they believe will give meaning and worth to life. While money can provide us with the means for worthwhile experiences, such as travel and time to enjoy our lives, it cannot provide us with the capacity to realize the worth of such experiences. What many fail to recognize is that having money cannot fulfill the internal self; searching externally to solve internal problems is a futile quest. While some of us may recognize this, very few of us are able to live it. Most of us simply love the myth that money solves problems; we ignore the reality that often it creates them.

Poverty Versus Luxury

At this point an important distinction needs to be made between not having any money (being poor) and having enough without approaching wealth (being comfortable). When we are poor, our concept of money is quite different from when we are adequately surviving but yearning for more. The problems that occur when we are poor are the basic problems of survival—of day-to-day existence. In many of these cases there are few available choices for change. The difficulties that occur are primarily those of continuing, staying alive, and surviving from one day to the next. These are substantially different problems from the ones we encounter when we are above the poverty line. As mentioned in the introduction, this book is not about surviving at the primary level of existence. Rather it focuses on a higher level of difficulties, the "luxury problems," or those that occur after our basic needs have been met.

For many in the world, poverty is not the problem but their way of life. For these people money is not a stressor but an unknown commodity. The poor of the world cannot imagine what problems would exist once there is sufficient wealth to provide for food, shelter, and basic survival needs. This book is for those of us who have achieved these things, or who have always had them, and have discovered that we are still encumbered, and perhaps even overwhelmed, by problems. In many ways our difficulties may be even more spiritually and emotionally severe than are those concerned with basic existence. This higher level of difficulties, then, may be the ones that we *need* to have—the problems that can teach us, develop us, and mature us. No one needs to be poor or to worry about everyday survival. No one benefits from a complete lack of choice or the inability to effect change. The impoverished condition would seem to be debilitating to the human spirit. Paradoxically, often it is not. Those who live in great poverty, here at home and abroad in third-world societies, are often more spiritual and balanced than many of us who live in luxury.

The Problem

We have one of the highest standards of living in the world, yet we do not have the highest quality of life. In spite of our luxury, depression ranks as our leading mental disorder. Stress-related diseases are on the rise, and suicides increase each year. We work harder and report less life satisfaction. We continue to spend more money on externals each year, yet we appreciate less and less. Most of us are looking at what we do not have and ignoring what we do. It seems we have not yet discovered the inverse relationship between possessions and contentment. When the amount of money we have does not make us happy or complete, we think we must make more. When we do not feel good about ourselves, we think that new clothes or a bigger house or a luxury car will help. For many of us it seems that the richer we become, the more impoverished are our spiritual sides. The more wealth, the less balance; the higher the standard of living, the greater the stress. The evidence is clear: After a certain point money does not solve problems, but instead creates them. Why, then, do so many of us continue on this quest for wealth even though we may recognize that it will not lead to balance and harmony?

The Training

The American culture is obsessed with making and spending money. In order to understand how this came to be, all we have to do is remember our history. America was not only the land of the "free and the brave," but also the nation that adopted the Protestant work ethic and its implications. From this came our predominant concept of success: the idea of working hard in order to achieve goals, usually materialistic ones. The Doing model teaches us that status is achieved through work. Money, then, becomes the ultimate symbol of status, our definitive measure of success and achievement. We can ask any ten people to define success, and chances are at least eight of them will mention material possessions. If we then ask them what they themselves most want to achieve in the next year, most likely money, or what it buys, will be mentioned. Thus money for most of us functions as the ultimate reward, the best prize, the supreme motivator. Money, we have been taught to believe, can fix almost anything. Once we have fallen off the Western model, either by rebellion or by economic conditions, as previously discussed, it is almost impossible to get back on. The "almost" is about those who can buy their way back on the model and back into society. We say that money cannot buy happiness, but we believe it surely can buy anything else that is important to have, and that having these things will lead to happiness.

We all know about the goodies money can buy and most of us yearn for at least one expensive item—a Mercedes, an Armani suit, an expensive vacation, a luxury home—in order to give us status, bolster our feelings of worth, or make someone notice and envy us. We can easily recognize the luxuries that money buys, but we may not be aware of other goals and desires that it indirectly fulfills. In this culture money *is* the illusion of power, and money often provides instant status. (This is not as true in other cultures, where breeding and tradition are valued above money. We have a tradition of respect for the nouveau riche in this country, while in many other countries the newly rich are frequently disdained.) Thus power and status define us as being important to others and quickly become a way of defining ourselves as successful. The Western model has taught us that we will get our satisfaction when we achieve our goals. It implies that money, power, status, and success will automatically make us happy and content. It has trained us to believe that life is in our control. That is why this model is dangerous: It perpetuates illusions and obsessions as the ways to achieve the contented life.

The Obsession

By now most of us are aware at some level that the idea that money can buy happiness or inner peace is a myth. We have seen too many movies, heard too many stories, been told about the lottery winners whose lives fall apart after they win. Furthermore many of us have learned not to discuss making lots of money as our primary goal in life. Why, then, are so many of us still stuck on the money-making treadmill? This quest is not about the money we require in order to survive, or even the extra money we need in order to be comfortable. Instead it refers to our desperate yearning for that one big break, our wish to win the lottery (we know that we will be different when *we* win!), or that unquenchable desire to make tons of money. If we really realize that money will not give us what we truly need, why do we continue to want it so much? Dream about it so often? Hope for it so desperately? Is this society so deprived when it comes to soul nurturing and true contentment that we resemble hungry little children, wanting more and more and more? Painful as it may be, the answer seems to be *yes*. We have been taught to want the things that money can buy in order to feed our needs for those things that money cannot buy. Even worse, we have been trained to feel deprived if we do not have *all* the things that money can buy. We have never been trained to say *enough!*

The Addiction

This obsession with always wanting more money has created a new type of addiction—the compulsive shopper. Spending money, buying new things, is no longer a pleasure or a recreational activity, but has moved into the realm of addiction and is no longer under the shopper's control. In the last few years a twelve-step program for addicted shoppers has been created, and the numbers afflicted are large. These are people who use shopping in the same way that drug, alcohol, and sex addicts do: as escape from themselves and the reality of their lives. This addiction is just as insidious as the others because it is self-destructive and can ruin the addict's life, not only financially but also with regard to relationships, stability, emotional health, and well-being. Shopping addicts buy things to try to feel better about themselves, stop the pain, deny their problems, and compensate for their insecurities. They buy things they do not want or need and will never use. They buy things because they are driven to do so and not because they want to do so. The sad fact is that what they are trying to buy cannot be purchased; the externals do not give us self-esteem and inner peace. As is true of all addicts, they want the "quick fix"; they want to feel good without having to do the internal work. These addicts can function as excellent role models for us; from them we can learn the lesson that we simply cannot purchase what we most need to obtain. Our possessions cannot give us what we really desire. We simply cannot shop for our Self. In the final analysis nothing external to us has any real life meaning.

The Paradox

The more we have, the more we take for granted. The things that we own eventually come to own us. Most of us do not think of comfort and external satisfaction as a luxury, but rather regard them as a right. Culturally we have been trained to believe that we have the right to whatever we want. We also believe that we are entitled to the best of what is available and that we deserve whatever good things we get. As Americans, most of us have traditionally been raised to perceive ourselves as the "lucky ones" in the world and the ones that can have whatever we desire as long as we are willing to work for it. Many of us have worked hard and obtained some degree of luxury in which we have reared our children. We have believed in working for what we get, and we may be surprised to discover that we have raised a new generation that does not believe in working hard to achieve a standard of living that they have always known. In other words the idea of working for what we have is being replaced by the concept of entitlement. For many of our children, a luxurious life is no longer considered a gift, but is instead perceived of as their right. This may be due to the fact that most of us take for granted that which is easily acquired or given. The one positive in the American work ethic—that we are a nation of hard workers—is being replaced by a generation of hard wanters. The concept that we work for what we want is being changed into the idea that merely wanting it is enough.

All of this is taking us in the wrong direction. We are moving even farther away from discovering what is really important. The next generation can quickly perceive that working hard and having things did not make their parents happy. Instead of going backward and questioning the premise that externals provide life satisfaction, they seem to have gone in the opposite direction. Many of them seem to have rejected the working part but kept the wanting part. The Doing model has failed to provide true life satisfaction; this model has placed worth and meaning in external things. Therefore it needs to be rejected as the model for discovering what is really important in life. However, to reject part of the model—the work part—and still keep the emphasis on the externals is not the way to find worth and life satisfaction. As a matter of fact the only thing that is positive about this model is the education and work emphasis. It may be a viable model for a small part of our lives—the work and doing sides—but it is an ineffective and destructive model for the rest of our lives—the balance, meaning, worth, and being sides.

The Reality

There is nothing wrong with money itself; it is a commodity for exchange and a necessary part of our lives. What is wrong is our attachment to it and our attributions of what it will do for us. It may be interesting to note that the familiar saying "Money is the root of all evil" is actually a misquotation. The actual phrase is "Love of money is the root of all evil." Money is simply money—it is not a measure of who we are, what we are worth, or our life success. When we perceive it as more than a commodity, we create destructive problems for ourselves. When we worship it, we lose our souls. When we quest after it, we lose our balance. When we place undue importance upon it, we lose our values. And when we focus all our energies upon it, we lose our spirits.

Money is *not* power, even though we have been trained to equate the two. Any power that can be purchased is not real power and will not last. Money is not freedom, even though we tend to perceive it as a means of being free. Freedom is a state of mind and as such cannot be bartered or bought. The exception to this may be real poverty; in this case money will enable us to survive longer, and perhaps better, but it will not make us freer. After a certain basic level of existence has been achieved, the possession of money tends to create stress and even more problems than it solves. Once we are fed, clothed, housed, and no longer destitute, money does not tend to function as a positive attribute. Humans quickly habituate to comfort and luxury; they easily become greedy. And this greed is the antithesis of joy. The following quotation by Kahlil Gibran is most appropriate in describing this process: "The lust for comfort, that stealthy thing that enters the house a guest, and then becomes a host, and then a master."

Finally, money is *not* worth, even though most of us confuse the two. Everything that is really important, after basic survival, is not dependent upon having money. Everything that money buys is external to the Self. Having wealth is not really important and is not especially difficult to obtain. Being happy, knowing who we are inside, finding peace, being real, developing self-esteem, practicing social interest (loving and sharing with others), and being spiritual (connected to God) are very important and much more difficult to attain. Far too often our quest for riches interferes with our quest for meaning. Money, then, becomes an enemy rather than a friend. The love of it reinforces our insecurities by placing our esteem onto externals and by valuing what is outside more than what is inside. Most of us desire money in order to impress others and to show them that we have achieved success. We want to look good, live well, and spend a lot so that others will perceive us positively. This is the domain of the weak ego: placing our worth on externals and judging ourselves through the eyes of others. We have been taught to believe that this is how to measure ourselves; we have been brainwashed by the myth of money.

The Solution

Becoming free; learning to be emotionally healthy; living in the moment; developing harmony, balance, and spirituality are the goals for problem-solving our so-called luxury problems. We would not have these luxury problems if we also did not have one of the highest standards of living in the world. Our system of working hard and being rewarded with money has given us our luxury; it has also given us some of our greatest stressors. Many of these difficulties are directly related to our expectations about the value of money. We do not have to relinquish our use for this commodity, but we need to give up any unrealistic desires for it. We need to refocus away from money and onto the real meaning of our lives. We need to reinvest the energy we have used to make money into making our own selves whole, balanced, and peaceful. We need to deflate our weak egos and inflate our self-esteem.

In order to begin, we first need to demystify the concept of money and dissociate it from our worth and value. We need to learn to go inside when previously we have gone outside. We need to ask ourselves, *Who exactly are we trying to impress?* If the answer is not our Selves, then why do it? We need to develop an awareness that our own souls are not at all impressed with what we wear, how we look, what we drive, or where we live. What impresses the soul cannot be purchased, is not easy to come by, and is not dependent in any way upon what impresses those around us. The soul is looking for character, integrity, morality, generosity—first to the Self and then to others—sensitivity, and compassion. None of these attributes are found in any external commodity, including money. Having them is not as simple as buying something, but once we have them, nothing else will ever be too difficult. Our life work is not easy, but unlike anything else we work for, this will last. And the price we pay will be small compared with what we receive. Nothing purchased with money will yield the same results.

IV ∽ Problem-Solving Money

1. Accepting

Accept the realization that money is just a commodity and not the definition of success. True success involves having goals other than making money, having money, spending money. Recognize the fact that money only satisfies the lowest ends of the life hierarchy—it only provides security and safety against some things. It cannot buy safety from life itself. Accept that you want to be much more than a money-making machine. Accept the premise that you want things that are not a part of the Western model, even though you may not yet know all that you want. Realize that at this moment you are learning, growing, and changing and that one of your biggest changes will be to give up the quest for money. You can do this if you believe that you already have everything you need in order to be balanced, whole, and content.

Begin to accept that the externals you desire are only externals; if you get them, you will soon tire of them. The things that will make a difference to you are not things you can buy. Accept that your weak ego is causing you to want more and more—to impress others, to match society's definition of success, or to achieve instant happiness. Your weak ego is a bad guide, for once you follow it, you will be caught on a never-ending treadmill of wanting, getting, and wanting more. Know that you are worth much more than anything that can be purchased. Your soul cannot be bought, your Self cannot be sold, and your worth and esteem are priceless. If something is worth having, it is not something that is easily obtained. Buying things is too easy; there is no challenge in exchanging one commodity (money) for another (external possessions). Accept that the real meaning of your life is not found in an exchange process but rather in a change process.

2. Letting Go

Let go of the myth of money, the fantasy of wealth, and the need for success as defined by external things. Let go of the idea that making more will make you better. Give up the illusion that money buys happiness, freedom, inner peace, or meaning. Let go of the idea that you alone can handle money differently than anyone else. You probably know others who have wealth and are not content. You have heard of the lottery winners whose lives fall apart. You have read about movie stars or celebrities whose lives are in turmoil in spite of their millions (or maybe because of them!). What makes you think you can handle great wealth any better? If you are not happy, balanced, practicing self-esteem, peaceful, and satisfied right now, what makes you believe that having lots of money will automatically change you? Solve your problems? Give you what you really need? You are responding to the illusion and the need for money that you have been trained to believe; let go of both. The training is pervasive, the myth is powerful, and the illusion is a compelling one; letting go will be very difficult. And yet there is no other way to free yourself of a very dangerous and destructive concept. The quest for wealth is dangerous because it takes you away from the truly important quest—your own search for your Self, your worth, your meaning. It is destructive because the love of money is a false love—you can easily lose everything that is good and loving about yourself by choosing the path of greed and avarice. You are so much more than a mere commodity—why sell your soul for something that is ultimately worthless?

3. Taking Responsibility

This is a hard step because so much of what you may feel and believe about money is due to your training. You cannot take responsibility for what you cannot control; therefore you were not responsible for what you were trained before you knew any better. However, now you know that money is not what you have always hoped or believed it was. Now you can recognize that achieving wealth will not mean you have achieved the real goals of your life. Once you are able to recognize this, you can begin to take responsibility for both your feelings about money and your choice of whether to define success externally or internally. Because you are the only one who has control over your own life, you are also the only one who can decide how much emphasis you want to place on monetary things.

You can choose to possess your own life, or you can choose to let your possessions own you. You can choose to spend your life making your Self more meaningful, or you can opt to spend your life making money. Whatever your choices, take full responsibility for them. If you choose to honor the myth, fantasy, and illusion about money, if you continue to have unrealistic expectations about what money can do for you, and if you decide to continue honoring money above all else, you are responsible. Yes, you will have lots of company because you will be following the model of this culture. Do not be surprised if this model leads you to depression, overwork, unnecessary stress, and unhappy relationships. If you look at others following the model, you will see these outcomes. You are not responsible for their choices; you are responsible for your own. Dare to be different; take the risk to try something new and much more powerful. Do not measure your life by something as frivolous as money. When you control your own life, rather than letting money control it, you will become real and internally powerful. Perhaps then you might also become a role model for those around you and help them change their destructive love of money.

4. Expressing Feelings

Perhaps you are feeling disillusioned, confused, angry, or sad. You are now being told that everything about money that you have been trained to expect is not true. You have a right to be unhappy. One of the most painful things you can ever do is lose your illusions. The myth of money is powerful and pervasive; expectations about love and money are the two strongest fantasies that exist. They are very similar in that both are supposed to satisfy you in your search for meaning. Both are purported to be the "quick fixes" in life. You have been told that when you are loved, you will be complete. You have also been told that when you possess wealth, you will be a success. Now you are being told that these are self-destructive illusions. You have a right to be upset. You may deny the reality that nothing outside of yourself, including money, will give your life worth or meaning. Know that the angrier you are, the more you have believed the illusion. The sadder you are, the more you may need the myth. And the more confused you are, the more dependent you have been on false expectations.

Express your feelings. Release your anger, your sadness, your confusion. Try not to analyze or rationalize your feelings—they are what they are and they need to be heard by you. Unexpressed feelings will block the potential for change; they will stop you from getting on with the real work of finding yourself. Get those feelings out so that you can move ahead. Cry your tears of frustration and lost hopes, yell your betrayal and rage at the world, allow yourself to be confused and uncertain. These feelings will pass—they always do once they are released. You have a lot to feel about; the Doing model has led you down the wrong path and you have to relearn how to Be and to relearn what is important. Before you can do so, you need to spend some time with your real self—your feeling self.

5. Forgiving

There may not be too much to forgive yourself for if you have believed the myth of money because you were a good student of a bad model. In this case you cannot blame yourself for what you have followed in good faith. Remember, you can only forgive yourself for what you have controlled—what you were responsible for. You may need to forgive yourself for desiring the "quick fix" and for hoping that your happiness and meaning could be purchased or obtained through external sources. What you have wanted is what you were taught to believe. The realization that all this is an illusion, unobtainable and unrealistic, is not something that occurs quickly or easily. Giving up this illusion takes time and effort. Forgive yourself for not wanting to do so. Forgive yourself and do it anyway.

You may need to spend more time forgiving this insecure society for what it has taught you. It may help you to do so if you realize that the lessons you have learned, the new awareness you have achieved, is part of your developmental progress and necessary for your growth. Turning away from the money myth is hard work. You cannot do this work unless you have first been caught up in the illusions. You cannot give up something that you have not first possessed. Therefore giving up the idea that money can make you happy or whole, successful or real, means that you had to adhere to these fantasies before you could release them. Forgive the world for making the adherence so easy and the releasing so difficult. Forgive others who may not be able to let go. Forgive your culture for teaching destructive values. Remember, the forgiveness you give is your gift to yourself. You enter this process to help yourself, to become free, and to become clean. This is something you do to better yourself.

6. Appreciating

Begin this step by appreciating that you are one of the lucky ones in that your problems with money are the luxury problems and not the difficulties of everyday sustenance and survival. Appreciate everything you now have—food in your body, a warm bed, a place to call home, a job or some means to continue your survival. And, above all, appreciate the fact that you have survived it all—all the craziness, the pain, the problems and the rat race. You are here and you are changing. That in itself is a lot to be thankful for.

You can appreciate the lessons you have learned about the worth of money even if you do not appreciate the teacher, the model. Everything you have learned has led you to this place where you can now begin to question. Look around you and see how many people are stuck on a never-ending, futile path defined by external success. At least you now know there is another way. You can be thankful that you have a way out, whenever you choose it. Appreciate the fact that you are able to learn, flexible enough to change, and smart enough to understand when something no longer works for you. You probably always knew, at some level, that money was not the worthwhile goal of life; now you can understand why this is true. If you have always desired money, now you can appreciate that there is much more in life to desire. If you have achieved money, now you can appreciate that there are far better things to go after. Be thankful that you have so many choices; all of them teach you what you need to know.

7. Rewarding

When working this step with this problem, make none of your rewards monetary. Only give rewards that have nothing to do with money or external things that money can buy. Reward yourself for recognizing that your meaning, esteem, and value have nothing to do with money. Reward yourself for recognizing the difference between your weak ego and your self-esteem. Your weak ego loves the quick and easy rewards, the things that impress others and have no intrinsic value. Your self-esteem requires rewards that have much deeper meanings and that nurture your soul. Being kind, especially when it is difficult; giving the gift of time, especially when you are rushed; being positive and empathetic; being loving and caring; sharing something of yourself that is hard to do; giving a smile; touching someone lovingly; listening; cooking something special; doing a kind deed; helping another; sharing your tears and joys; telling your deepest secret; being there for another; being there for yourself; patting another on the back for a good job; patting yourself; giving a sincere compliment; doing any one of a million acts of kindness—all of these are wonderful rewards. These are the things that make life worthwhile and that are remembered long after the purchased gifts have been forgotten. These are the things we need to do and to receive; these are the gifts of life. Remember, when you reward others, you are also rewarding yourself. And when you reward yourself, you are also rewarding God.

Life can only be understood backwards,
but it must be lived forwards.

—Søren Kierkegaard

V ∽ Time

There is a wonderful concept in the East: Money is replaceable and unlimited, whereas time is irreplaceable and limited. In the West we seem to have reversed this idea. We believe that there will always be more time but never enough money. As a result time in this culture tends to be considered a commodity and not a particularly valued one. We generally think of time as something that is ours to own and in our control. We speak of having "time on our hands" or "not enough time to do what we want." We talk about "killing time" and "spending time," and we act as if we have "all the time in the world." We "take our time" and "use time" as needed. Because we have learned our concept of time from a linear model, it is no surprise that we have a linear concept of time. We tend to perceive time as stretching out in front of us or behind us as a straight line, despite Einstein's theory that time is not linear. The Doing model has trained us to value what we do with time rather than to value the concept of time itself. Because death is not represented on this model, there is very little awareness or real understanding of time being limited. Furthermore the Western model does not deal with any limitations that are out of our control. Therefore the concept of time has to be reduced to something that can be managed and controlled. The model does this so well that it is difficult to realize exactly how dangerous these illusions are.

The Reality of Time

One reality about time is that we know very little about it and have only a paradoxical way of controlling it. We do not own time, and indeed time may well own us. Other realities are that time is not linear, not one-dimensional, and not a commodity at all. Time is not a place or a state or even a process. The invention of the clock, by measuring time, gave us the illusion that it was now in our control. The clock and the calendar defined time by seconds, minutes, hours, days, and years, and we forgot that we constructed such measurements for our own convenience. In doing so we also forgot the interrelationship between time and nature. If we travel around the world, we immediately see how these measurements are just that and not the answers to what time is. Jet lag painfully confronts us with the reality that we do not control or even understand time. When we fall in love, we will experience an altered state of time. Time has not changed (has it?), but our perceptions of it most certainly have. We perceive time and believe that our perceptions are reality. They are, for us at that moment, but these perceptions are only temporal constructions of reality and not the answers for everyone. The Doing model has taught us that these perceptions are the reality of time. It has taught us to "use, lose, waste, own, manage, spend, save" and otherwise control time in order to perpetuate the perception of time in our control. And by doing so it has taught us that time is of little worth or consequence. One critical reality is that time is all we have, and it may be the most important facet of our being. We cannot exist if we do not have the time in which to do so. We cannot be if we are not being in time. Time and life are synonymous and personally interchangeable—our life and our time mean the same—and both cannot be replaced once they are gone.

The Importance of Time

If we can spend one day with those who are dying and who realize that the end of their lives, their time, is quickly approaching, we will change our concept of time. (We are all dying, but we do not know this until our perception of death becomes our immediate reality.) The meaning that time has for these people, who are about to lose their immediate perception of time, is probably the best, most accurate definition of time. For those aware of imminent death, time is everything. No minute is not precious. They will try to hold on to every second of time, even if it is painful to do so. Ask them about time being replaceable and money not. If they have the strength, they will probably laugh. Most of them will tell us how their regrets all have to do with time and not valuing it enough; very few will have regrets about money. They may also tell us what to do with our lives and uniformly they will tell us to be aware, appreciative, and to value and really live in the time that is available to us. They will show us how little we own or control time. If possible, we can try not to pass up this most valuable learning experience. It is a tragedy that the Western model teaches us nothing about time until it is too late to use the information. However, we can learn about it while we still have the time to enjoy and benefit from our new awareness.

Real Time

We know that there is no life without time. We do not know if time exists without some form of life. We know that we cannot be outside of time and we also know that the only time that is ours is the moment. Yes, we have lived in the past and we remember parts of that living process, but we can do absolutely nothing about what has already happened. It is over, gone, finished, dead, and totally out of our control. There is only one thing that we can constructively do with our past, and that is to learn from it. We can do many destructive things with it, such as feeling guilty about it, trying to relive it, regretting it, punishing ourselves with it, using it as an excuse for present behaviors, or trying to change it. None of these things are possible and they only function to keep us away from the "real" time, the present. These behaviors actually keep us out of time and are therefore dangerous and self-defeating. We can learn from our past, but in order to do so, we must first be able to let it go. We must be realistic about the past—it is time that is gone forever. It is no longer our time.

Neither is our future our time. The Doing model fails to teach us this critical reality. As a matter of fact the model teaches us just the opposite—that we have all the time we need to accomplish our goals if we follow the prescribed path. Dreams, ambitions, and goals are always future oriented. Once we have achieved them, they become our past. The American view is future oriented. What is ahead has always been more important than what is here now. Our culture, more than many others, puts great emphasis on the future, and values the long-term perspective. It is interesting to note that this is an American trait rather than a Western one, as many countries in what we consider the Western world put far less emphasis on the future.

Living in the Present

Just as guilt lives in the past, anxiety lives in the future. Neither one of these negative perceptions exists in the present. For in the present we are busy creating what will soon become our past; we are not as anxious about what we are actually doing as we are when we think about doing it. The doing of the thing overrides the feelings of guilt or anxiety. These usually occur later, when we are thinking either backward or forward. If we could only stay in the present and live in the moment, we would never have time to experience guilt or anxiety. We would be free.

Living in the moment is similar to Being in that it is something that is already occurring. However, until we become aware of it, the process of Being does not have meaning for us. And once we do become aware of the importance of being in the moment, the process, which is a natural one and already ongoing, becomes most difficult. This sounds a bit crazy, but the absurdity exists because we have never been taught to be aware of what we are naturally doing all the time. We have not been trained to recognize the simple, important components of living well. Most of us have used our time trying to cope with the difficulties of life. We have been told that we must overcome our problems and win at life. We have learned how to master time rather than to honor it. We were never trained to know how very precious time is to each of us and that there will never be enough time to learn everything we can about Being.

Time and Being

As mentioned, living in the moment and Being are a lot alike. Actually they are exactly alike because they are the same thing. Being means living in this moment in time. When we are aware of the moment, we are Being. How can we not be in the moment? We can also ask, How can we not be? The answer to both is exactly the same: by not being aware—actively and consciously aware—of what we are right now. Being fully alive means being consciously aware of our lives as they are occurring. This awareness of what we are doing or not doing at all times is critical to the process of Being, or living in the moment. We cannot take ourselves out of this moment in time and be fully alive. Yet most of us have been trained to do just that. It is no wonder that so many of us complain that we do not really feel alive and that we need drugs, therapies, and other people in order to deal with the pains and problems of life. When we say that we cannot cope or we feel hopeless and helpless, chances are that we are not dealing with the present moment, but are instead consumed with either our past or our future, or, God help us, both at the same time. In other words we are focusing our awareness on time that is out of our control. When we do so, we feel out of control ourselves.

Awareness of the Moment

It may be an oversimplification to define mental health by the degree to which we are aware of the moment, but the following examples will help to demonstrate exactly how critical the concept of time is to our health. Those who have lost all awareness of time are labeled psychotic; they are out of touch with reality and not able to connect themselves to the moment. Those who bounce between the states of having some awareness of themselves in the moment and having none and who tend to live most of their lives in the past are the personality disorders, or what used to be called neurotic. Those who can separate past, present, and future and bounce around between them fairly equally and who have a fairly consistent sense of themselves in the moment are "normal" (in this culture). Finally, those who are actively and consistently aware of the moment and who spend most of their time in the present are the sages, gurus, or wise ones. Some people might call these latter ones crazies. Those people who would label them as such are probably the same people defined as the successes of the Doing model and are the ones who are most likely to be threatened by the concept of being rather than doing.

Thus our mental health to a large degree depends on our realistic awareness of time and our ability to live in the present. This may seem somewhat obvious, but if so, why do we have so much difficulty living in the moment? Why is too much of our focus often on the future? When we look at our linear, goal-oriented Doing model, we will instantly have the answers. These answers will help explain why our society dwells on the future. Our culture values and strongly rewards a futuristic orientation. Our government continues to spend future earnings and does not want to be held responsible for what is going on at this moment. Politicians know that most present difficulties can be blamed on the past regime; they will not be held accountable in the future. After all, what the politicians do now will not be seen until a future time, and frequently this is a far distant time. Imagine for a moment what would occur if the entire society focused for one day on that day only. Suppose everyone looked at the problems of this day and actively worked on only these problems. This may be unrealistic, but it would be incredibly powerful. And a great number of our present problems that are supposedly unsolvable could be resolved.

The Problem with the Future

Of course there are some powerful advantages to having plans for the future, and it would be impossible to live without some future orientation. But there is a matter of degree to be considered, and our culture is far too future oriented, at the expense of the present. Most Americans sacrifice the present in the hopes of satisfying future goals. They are overworking now in order to enjoy their efforts later. And often, later never comes. Our reality does not exist in the future. None of us can guarantee that we will have a future. And if we do, we still cannot control it, define it, or change it. We can only do these things right now, in the present. If we as a country could only reverse the focus and spend the time on the actual present that we currently do on the future, we might be amazed at how much more harmonious and in control we could be. However, this is unrealistic; this society and our cultural values are not soon going to relinquish the focus on the future. But there is nothing stopping each of us from changing our own individual time frame. Just because we have been taught to be future oriented and just because we have previously been goal driven does not mean that we have to continue in this way. Our time, at this moment, and our lives, right now, are in our control. If we want more harmony, more balance, and more control over our lives, we can have these when we practice being in the moment.

Wasting Time

Our training has taught us many ways and reasons to stay out of the moment. We usually have many excuses for problems with time, but we may not yet realize how many of these difficulties stem from our own doings. We create some of these problems when we focus our valuable time on trying to impress others. Any time we spend trying to please, cater to, or change others is time we lose taking care of ourselves. It becomes wasted time, because we have no control over others. This may be contrary to what we have learned—that it is important to cultivate high opinions from other people and to impress others, especially those who are useful to us. If we think about how much time in our lives we have spent trying to please others, making them like us, fostering good impressions, or trying to influence them, we will quickly realize how powerful is our training. If we are appalled and cannot bear to think of all the time we have wasted trying to please or control others, join the club. The Western model has taught us to do so, and the time we have spent impressing others reflects how good a student we have been.

We may already have learned that we cannot control anyone else's feelings. If others like us or even love us, if they are impressed by us, it probably has more to do with where they are at this time than anything we may be doing. If we stop and think about this for ourselves, we will realize that we may not know all the reasons we like or love other people, but once we do, our feelings are in our control and not in theirs. For instance they may do things we do not like or admire, but we still care for them. Our admiration for others is also much more dependent on where we are than on what they are doing. People cannot impress us if we are not in an impressionable place. The same holds true when we reverse this process and consider what others are thinking or feeling. As a matter of fact, trying to impress others often has the opposite effect, for they may perceive us as desperate or working too hard. We can all stop using time in a futile manner if we stop trying to do things to impress others. Instead we can become actively aware of our own relationships with time. We can begin by taking the time to please ourselves. We can take care of our own needs. When we do so, we are living in the moment and focusing our awareness and attention on our own Being. This prevents any further waste of time.

Confusing Importance with Time

Another problem with time occurs when we confuse a sense of urgency with a sense of importance. Workaholics frequently do this. Our society seems overrun by these rushing, out-of-breath, busy-busy-busy, compulsive, obsessive, stressed-out type A individuals. Many of these unfortunates are terribly insecure about their own worth and value. To them, looking overworked equates to being important. Never having enough time translates into being indispensable. Our culture reinforces always "doing" and "using time productively," and these constructs are reflected by these image-conscious overachievers.

One small example of this are the people who are *always* talking on their car phones. It seems as if their time is just too precious for merely driving a car. Perhaps their need to be perceived as significant or special by others is achieved by driving and talking at the same time, thereby conveying the message of extreme importance. As a result their attention is not focused, and they are not doing anything with concentration, neither driving nor talking nor impressing anyone else. There is something quite sad about those who are or who try to appear to be "too busy." There is something even sadder about those who look on this as a positive state. Unfortunately we are all familiar with the large numbers of sad, insecure, and depressed individuals in this society. Never being in the moment is a certain recipe for depression and insecurity.

Defining Productive Time

This culture, by virtue of the Doing model, has taught us to focus on accomplishment. Thus time is considered productive when it leads to a finished product, a met goal, or an effective outcome. Time that is not used to produce an end result is not considered important. Time spent on relationships and their development is not as valued in this culture as time spent on achievement. From this perspective we have learned to view other cultures with some disdain because they use time differently and, to us, "unproductively." Cross-cultural research shows many examples of the difficulties encountered by Americans trying to do business in more relationship-oriented cultures. We have learned to get to the bottom line as quickly as possible, to make the deal and to get on with the business at hand. Many other cultures value the time spent getting to know one another, enjoying being involved, and sharing a relaxed meal or leisurely trip with others. To them just being together is an important part of the business process. In contrast, Americans have learned to be driven by efficiency, to be productive, and to use time "well," which means to accomplish the goals. In other words our model has not trained us to value the time spent on developing relationships. And so, for the most part, we do not. This use of time reflects our training and leads to our most common relationship problems, in all arenas of our lives.

Another problem occurs when productivity is confused with the amount of time spent on the task. Workaholics are frequently guilty of spending a lot of time working but actually not being very productive. Our model lends itself beautifully to using time at work as an escape mechanism from other areas of our lives. If we are having relationship problems, it is easy to hide from them by working all the time. We can even blame these problems on our work and thus escape spending time resolving them. Because this culture is obsessed with how we spend our time and because we have learned that time spent at work is usually viewed positively, work time can then become all-of-life time for those looking for quick and easy ways out of major life dilemmas. When we are working all the time, or too much of the time, we need to ask ourselves what we are avoiding by doing so. At the very least we are avoiding spending time with ourselves. How are we going to know that we are fully alive, really here and living in the moment, if we do not dedicate some time to ourselves? Ultimately there is nothing more productive than knowing who we are and having good relationships, first with ourselves and then with others.

Learning the Value of Time

No matter how important we may think we are at work, we are not important at all if we do not have a good relationship with ourselves and with those we love. We need time in which to do these critical life-enhancing things. The model has not taught us that our lives are *now,* right at this moment, and not just our work or what we do. The model has not reinforced the reality that we have a limited amount of time in which to spend our lives and that this time is very precious and quickly gone. And most importantly the model has definitely not taught us that doing is not always the best use of time. It has not trained us how to Be or the value of Being. The model has not dealt with these issues, but that does not mean that we cannot take the time to learn them. We are learning them right now. There may never be a more valuable use of our time than the time it takes to refocus our conception of time and to change our perceptions about the meaning and value of our lifetimes.

Now is a good time to learn a paradox about controlling time: Time will always control us when our goals are to control it. There will never be enough time if we live our lives trying to master the concept of time. Instead we will either feel driven by time or we will suffer from never having enough time or, conversely, always having too much time on our hands. But when we let go of our need to control time and focus solely on the present, we become actively aware of the moment: We discover that we have complete control over it and ourselves in this present moment. We need to learn to let go in order to let be, and then we will have it all, including the time that we need.

Living the Moment

How do we begin to live the moment? If this sounds like a ridiculous question, recognize that this is because we have been well trained by the Doing model. The answer to this question may be one of the most difficult things we can ever learn. The answer is simple, but the practice of it is not easy. We can begin to live the moment by becoming aware of the moment. We need to stop whatever we are doing, thinking, and feeling and merely focus on our breathing. If we attempt to do this, we will soon discover exactly how difficult it is. Why should it be so hard to think about our breathing and nothing else? Because we have been trained never to stop everything else and do such a mindless thing. How unnecessary it is, we have learned, to pay attention to ourselves and our breathing. This is something that happens without our active awareness, so why should we worry about it or pay attention to it? After all, we have been taught, there are better and more important things to do with our time. And so, when we do try to stop and pay attention, we may find that we cannot.

Our minds usually start working overtime. We will quickly

become flooded with thoughts. It is as if our minds are two-year-olds who have just discovered that their parents are ignoring them. This cannot be tolerated and the attention must be regained. To resolve this, we need to open the floodgates and watch the thoughts come pouring through. And if our minds are working overtime, so also are our feelings. Stopping everything else and focusing on our breath may feel stupid, strange, or awkward. We may feel that we cannot breathe perfectly, and therefore it becomes more comfortable not to pay attention to our breath. We may feel that this is beneath us; of course we can pay attention to only our breathing, but we do not want to at this time. We may think that any time that we desire, we will be able to do so. This is a common denial of the difficulty of this exercise. Please do not be fooled. We only have now in our control. If we do not want to do it now, when will we ever want to do it? Our bodies may not cooperate in this change of focus and attention. We may be trying to focus only on our breath and our bodies may start cramping, itching, or feeling uncomfortable. We may have an uncontrollable urge to tap our feet or strum our fingers or lick our lips or scratch somewhere. We may want to cough or sneeze or have the hiccups. Our bodies may want our attention on it and not on our breathing.

Breathing Is Being

All of these things happen to all of us when we first try to focus our attention on only our breathing. Or when we actively try to be aware of the moment. They do not happen to young children or to those taught from a different perspective about what is important. Nothing is more important to each of us than our breathing. It is our sign of life, our mechanism for staying alive, and our metaphor for life and death. Each breath we take in is a rebirth, a new beginning, an affirmation of continuing life. Each breath we let out is a death, an ending, a letting go of life. And what we are breathing in and out is more than air; it is time. Our life *time* is composed of millions and millions of separate breaths, each one a complete cycle of taking in and letting out, beginning and ending, living and dying. While it is true that we are not fully alive just by breathing, it is also true that we are not fully alive if we never focus on this incredible process and never become aware of our breath in the moment.

We can try it again. We do not have to try to breathe perfectly. We cannot, because there is no such thing as a perfect breath. The fact that we are breathing is enough. (If we are not sure about this, we can ask anyone with emphysema or asthma.) We do not have to try to breathe better than anyone else. This is not a contest. (If we do find that we are comparing our breathing to someone else's, this will tell us a lot about our training.) We do not have to worry if our breathing is loud or soft. This is not a social occasion. In other words we can breathe without judgment. It may help to put our attention on the tip of the nose and notice the breath going in (it feels cool) and coming out (it feels warmer). We can take long, deep breaths and notice how it feels in our noses, in our lungs, in our abdomens. We can focus on the feeling of full and then on the feeling of empty. We can take deep breaths in and hold them. Then we can let our entire breath out and hold it. Next we can take short, choppy breaths and let them out quickly. We can play with our breathing. We can take a long breath in and let it out quickly. Next time let it out very slowly. We can experiment with how many different ways we can breathe. We can have fun with this exercise. It is not brain surgery. But it is life and death! We can control our breathing. We can control the time in which we are breathing. We may notice that now we are fully alive, fully aware, and that it is no longer hard or difficult. We may notice that our bodies feel more relaxed. When we are deep-breathing, our bodies always go into a more relaxed state. It is impossible to feel tense or anxious when we are focusing on our deep, steady breathing. This is better medicine than any pill.

Being Is Life

Our minds may still be acting like spoiled two-year-olds, demanding our attention in every possible way. We can do exactly what we would do to our little children as loving parents: We can tell our minds to please go play in the other room for a while and that we will soon come join them and give them all the attention they need. And when we find that our thoughts come tumbling back in to divert our attention from our breath, again we can ask them to go play in the other room and tell them we will attend to them shortly. This method works. Getting mad or frustrated or trying to ignore what is happening never works because all these activities end up diverting our attention from our breathing. They do what they are trying to do: They stop us from being. We can do the same kinds of things with our feelings: Let them float on by. If we are feeling uncomfortable, acknowledge the feeling briefly, let it go, and get back to focusing on our breathing. If we are feeling stupid or strange, we can reassure ourselves that this is good for our weak egos and focus once again on our breath. We need always to bring our focus, gently and lovingly, back to our breath. We can let our feelings float up and away; it may help to imagine that they are helium-filled balloons, briefly watch them, and then return to the breath.

After a short while our thoughts will not intrude as frequently, our minds will clear, our feelings will subside, and our breathing will become more and more interesting. If our bodies act up, we can attend to them briefly and return to focusing on our breathing. We may need to scratch our itches, move our cramped limbs, cough, clear our throats, wiggle our toes, move our fingers, or do whatever we have to do as quickly as we can, and return our focus to our breath. Our bodies will give up trying to divert our attention more quickly than our minds will, because our bodies are actively involved in the breathing process. Our minds are not involved at all. When we can achieve breathing without distraction, then we are in a meditative state. We are also in a very relaxed state. We are in the moment, we are actively being, and we may be surprised to discover that this feels natural and comfortable. What started out as a mindless activity has become one of the most mindful things we can do. Each time we practice our deep breathing, we will discover that it is easier to return to the state of relaxation and well-being. This process becomes very natural after a short while. If possible, try to practice every day. The time we spend Being is the time of our lives.

Once we discover how to Be, we will simultaneously discover that there is plenty of time. "There's a time for some things and a time for all things; a time for great things, and a time for small things," wrote Cervantes. Once again there is paradox: Letting go is being, being in the moment is living, living is appreciating time, and time cannot be controlled but can only be lived. The secret to living is to learn to let go; the secret to being is living the moment. Life is about the awareness of the moment, while death is about letting go. When we breathe, we do both. Perhaps our own breathing is the best metaphor for what we need to learn about living and dying.

VI ∽ Problem-Solving Time

1. Accepting

When you think about the problems you have with your time, try to separate them into those that are necessary and those that are unnecessary. Necessary problems with time are those that you probably cannot change or control or resolve. These are the problems you must accept in order to learn from them. They are the problems that are important for you to have at this time in your life. The ones that are unnecessary are probably the ones that come from your training or from the Doing model. These are the problems that you do not have to accept, since you can change them, move beyond them, or solve them.

Begin the acceptance process by realizing that despite your training you cannot control time. Accept the fact that your life time is limited and that you do not know the limits. This means that you must accept that you are mortal and you will die. (If this is painful or difficult, you may want to turn to the section on death.) Next accept the fact that what you do with your life time is now your responsibility and that even though you cannot control time, you can make some choices that will allow you to make the best of the time you have. Accept the simple fact that the only time that is really important to you is the present; the past and the future are never, and will never be, in your control. The only thing you can control is what you do in the moment; even then you are not really controlling time, but you are controlling your relationship with the moment. Accept that this is the most you can ever do.

Accept the fact that your training has put you at war with the concept of time. Stop fighting and trying to change time. Learn that even though you do not know much about the concept of time, you do know what you need to about the moment. This moment, and only this one, is yours to do with as you choose. Accept that it is your choice how you spend this moment and that this moment ultimately becomes your life. Accept that the process of being is very different from doing and that learning how to consciously Be is very difficult. Finally accept that you must learn to live the moment in order to really live at all. Practice being in the moment. Practice being aware of only the present. Stop time-jumping and make peace with the time you are in. Know that this moment is all you really have and that it is enough.

2. Letting Go

Begin by looking at your unnecessary problems with time. These may include fighting time, denying it, obsessing over it, or using it as a defense or excuse for failure to live in the moment. These problems are manifested by chronic lateness or earliness, constant rushing, procrastinating, always needing to appear busy, becoming depressed, or being out of touch with reality. Let them go. It does not matter where they came from or that they have now become habits, you still need to let them go. They do not work for you, or they would not be problems. If your problems with time are about your image (spending time trying to impress others), you can resolve them by spending time with yourself and becoming self-secure so that you no longer need a facade. You may want professional help to do this; being in therapy counts as spending time on yourself.

If your problems with time are about achievement and accomplishment, think about what you really want to be at the end of your life. Imagine that today is the last day of your life and that you will die tonight. Now, what do you want to achieve today? What accomplishment will make you feel your life has been a personal success? What can you do about this? Do not wait until the final end of your life, because you may not be fortunate enough to know when it will occur. You may not have enough time to do what you want to do if you procrastinate. Begin now at this moment to do what is most important for you. Put down this book and write or call or talk to someone you love or whatever you need to do so that when you go to bed tonight, you will feel that you have accomplished your life today.

Let go of the idea that your life exists in the future. It does not. Also let go of trying to relive the past. You cannot do that either. Let go of your self-destructive needs always to be doing something. Your worth is not dependent on your productivity or your activities. Even though you have probably been taught that these are the important components of living, now you are aware that they will not fulfill you. You have been cheated out of much of your valuable time. Do not allow this to continue. Also let go of trying always to prove yourself. Relax. Be. Just be. It is difficult at first, but the more you practice being, the easier it becomes and the more you will love it. Let go of this society's obsession with time—it will only drive you mad and waste your precious time. Finally, let go of the Western confusion between time and money; remember that time is by far the more valuable of the two. Time is everything and money is nothing when you reach the end of your life. You will probably always have enough money to survive, but you will never have enough time if you waste it in the pursuit of the externals.

3. Expressing Feelings

When you think about time, what do you feel? Pay attention to your feelings. When you wake up in the morning and think about the day ahead of you, what do you feel? This day is not just time that you will go through—this day ahead of you is your life. It is your reality. Yesterday is no longer yours and tomorrow is unattainable; today is it. How does that make you feel? You can learn a great deal about your life if you pay attention to your feelings about the time that you are currently living—this moment.

Remember, your feelings are different from your thoughts.

Your thoughts reflect your experience, training, image, and ego. Your feelings more accurately reflect the real you in this moment. You cannot control either your thoughts or your feelings, but you can control what you do with them. You have been trained to pay too much attention to your thoughts and too little to your feelings. Reverse this. Whatever you are feeling is real, it is you at this moment, and it will not last. It is a temporary state. You can let your feelings teach you by paying attention to them. Express to yourself whatever you may be feeling and then let the feeling go.

If your predominant feeling about time is frustration, know that this is a combination of a thought and a feeling. Frustration is generally composed of a feeling, such as anger or sadness, melded to a thought, such as "I should not be feeling this" or "I am incompetent." Frustration usually reflects insecurity. It means you are mad at yourself for what you are or are not; it reflects negative judgments. It means that your weak ego is in control. Try to separate the thought from the feeling. Recognize that the thought comes directly from your training and put it aside or let it go. Express the feeling that underlies your frustration. If it is anger, be angry. If it is sadness, be sad. Whatever the feeling, let it out. Then let it go. It is amazing how natural change becomes when you can separate your thoughts from your feelings and express the underlying feeling. It is much easier to get on with the process of life when your feelings are allowed to occur, be expressed, and then released.

If your predominant feeling about time is pressure or stress, know that again you have combined a thought with a feeling and that underneath the pressure is probably the feeling of fear.

You most likely feel pressured or stressed when you are trying to achieve something, impress someone, or attempt the impossible or unrealistic. You are not a superman or superwoman. Your anxiety (also a combination of fear and insecurity) tells you that you are working against yourself. You are spending your time in a self-destructive manner. Life will never be free of stress or without some pressure, but if this is the predominant mode of your life, something is very wrong. Express your fear. Recognize your anxiety. Stop trying to be more than human. Take care of your precious time; in the end it is all you have.

4. Taking Responsibility

As previously mentioned, you do not have to take responsibility for things over which you have no control. The Western model and your training from this model have not been your responsibility, up to this minute. Before you knew that there was another model for your life, you could not be held accountable for being a good student on a bad model. But now you can. Now, right now, you are responsible for how you choose to spend your time. You are in control of your priorities, your choices, and your behaviors. If you choose to continue using your time in the pursuit of unrealistic goals, a never-ending supply of money, status, and an impressive image, you are responsible. You know that there are other things you can be doing with your time. Yes, you probably have to work in order to survive. But do you have to work as much as you currently do? Are you happy with your life today? Are there things that you must change, want to change, or need to change in order to feel good about yourself? Are you spending all your time producing and doing or are you spending your time meaningfully? Remember, these are rarely the same thing.

A few years ago time management was a hot topic and seemed to be the answer to many problems. The emphasis today, both within organizations and in dealing with life-development issues, has shifted away from this topic, probably because trying to "manage" time does not lead to a balanced or emotionally healthy life. The concept of time management comes right off the Doing model. Who are you managing time for? Are you trying to be more effective, productive, and goal oriented? The problem with the Doing model will not be solved by doing more, doing it better, or doing it faster. The faults inherent in this model can only be countered by finding an alternative model. This is because the Doing model is very strict and inflexible with its goals and definitions: Success means being future oriented, achieving, doing things effectively, winning, impressing others, not making mistakes, and always working toward your goals. If you do not follow this, then you cannot be a success; you will be defined as a failure. When you pay more attention to the present than you do to the future, you are off the model. If you pay more attention to your own needs than you do to your image, then you are also off the model. Please jump off this crazy-making model. Learn about being. Take full responsibility for doing so. Take your life into your own hands and spend it carefully and well.

5. Forgiving

You cannot forgive yourself for what you learned from your previous training. It is very difficult to forgive an entire society for a faulty training program, especially when the society does not want to acknowledge the blame. You can only forgive that which has been rightfully blamed. You will only be wasting your time if you try to forgive a culture that will perceive you as insane for wanting to be off the model. You cannot change the society or the model. You can only change yourself and your needs to be on the Doing model.

If you decide to take some, just some, of your life time into your own hands, and if you practice being just a few moments each day, you will have nothing to forgive yourself for. Just do it. If you decide to wait and to waste more of your life, then you may well have to forgive yourself later on. You may want to consider this: Five minutes a day of being is worth twenty-four hours of forgiving. Which seems more effective? More productive? More sensible and beneficial? What is stopping you?

6. Appreciating

Begin this exercise by appreciating that you still have time to do something about your life. It is never too late to change. Recognize that your discomfort and problems with time have led you to this place and time. Reflect on the fact that your experiences on the Doing model have not solved your needs and desires to be whole and healthy. Appreciate how hard you tried to follow the model, how much you believed, how much effort you expended, and how much time you spent. Now you do not ever have to do so again. Appreciate exactly what you have learned and get on with learning something new. And do not forget to appreciate the fact that your life, your change, your time are now in your hands. And when you do spend time Being, when you work on yourself, and when you satisfy your own needs, appreciate yourself. You are doing something for yourself—you are off the old model and on a new one—you have expanded your repertoire and created new options for your life—appreciate your efforts.

Appreciate all the frustration, the pain, the anxiety, and the pressure that have been in your past. You will surely experience all of these feelings and worries again, but never quite in the same way and perhaps not to the same degree. Your problems with time and your difficult feelings about yourself, your life, and your goals have all taught you so much. For one thing they have taught you what does *not* work for you. This is a huge lesson. They have also taught you not to keep doing something that does not work; doing more does not make it work better. You have already learned that the model is not about truth, justice, fairness, or equality. Your pain has taught you that following the model does not solve your major problems. (As a matter of fact the model creates many more problems than it resolves.) Appreciate all this knowledge and awareness. Anything you learn that helps you change, mature, and let go of negative and destructive ideas is worthwhile information; it means that you have not wasted all your time. Remember, life is about learning, and everything you have done is part of your personal lesson.

7. Rewarding

Now is the time to learn one of the great paradoxes about time: the more time you take to help yourself *be,* the more time you will have in order to *do.* This may not seem logical, but defining time is not a logical endeavor. When you put all your emphasis on doing, there never seems to be enough time. However, when you put your emphasis on being, time seems to open up, expand, and become sufficient. Perhaps this occurs because the Doing model teaches you to think only in terms of what time can do for you, rather than what you can be in the time you have. Recognizing this may be one of the most rewarding things you will ever do. It is very clear that what you need to learn to live well is not found on this Western model. It is also clear that the Being model, which has no stated goal or purpose, is the one that will satisfy your quest for meaning. Ironically the rewards you seek are not on the model that purports to be reward oriented. Another wonderful paradox!

Reward yourself for Being. If you do nothing else in your lifetime but this, you will probably have done enough. In the final analysis this may be one of the most important lessons you will ever learn.

*The universe is change; our life is
what our thoughts make it.*

—MARCUS AURELIUS ANTONINUS

VII ⌁ Changes and Choices

Whether we are consciously aware of it or not, change is the fabric of our lives. We ourselves are continually and constantly changing—our physical bodies, our minds, our feelings, and our spiritual sides are never static or permanent. Our environment is also in a state of never-ending change—nature, weather, time, and seasons are composed of both cyclical and unpredictable changes. Everything we are involved with or interested in is in a state of flux; science, business, politics, the economy, education, technology, the arts—music, literature, theater, dance, film, and television—all reflect change. Life is a process of constant movement; every day is different from the one before or the one to come. Every individual person differs slightly from day to day. There are very few permanent or immutable parts of ourselves or our lives. We change, others change, and the world is forever changing. Why, then, is change one of our major stressors? Perhaps the answers are found when we consider what we try to do with the concept of change. Usually we try to control or direct it, or we try to force, cause, or be responsible for its occurrence. When we are involved in creating or forcing change, we do so through making decisions or choices. The process of change is not in our control—we cannot halt change and we cannot *not* make decisions. Everything we do, in same manner, is due to a choice we have made, whether it be inadvertent or deliberate. Therefore we are always going to have problems dealing with change and making choices. We are always going to be coping with the stresses caused by them. Thus they become necessary problems and function to help us learn to be problem solvers.

Stress and Change

If we were asked to consider the changes that cause the most stress to our lives, we would probably first think of the traumatic or destructive ones. For example the death of a loved one would clearly be a major life stressor and would be perceived as a negative change. It might be somewhat surprising to discover that positive changes can also produce great stress. Research on life stress has shown that marriage, marital reconciliations, pregnancy, retirement, and new jobs all are high stressors. Two psychiatrists, Thomas Holmes and Richard Rahe, developed the Social Readjustment Rating Scale, which measures in Life Change Units the amount of stress that occurs with specific changes. The scale is used to compute an annual stress score in order to predict the likelihood of stress-related illness: The higher the Life Change Units, the greater the possibility of sickness. It ranks forty-three life stressors and assigns each a numerical value. One interesting feature of this measure is that it clearly demonstrates that any significant life change, whether it be positive or negative, produces stress. It lists those changes that are a part of normal life and shows that even things we want and try to achieve, such as more money, more responsibility at work, a new house, beginning or ending school, vacations and holidays, revising our personal habits, or changing our eating habits all produce significant amounts of personal stress.

Therefore if change is an unavoidable and necessary aspect of life, then so is stress. To put it simply, life is change and change is stressful. Problems occur when we resist, deny, or rebel against the realities of life. We need to learn that no matter how much we try to do to be secure, no matter how safe or important we believe we are, nor how much responsibility we try to assume over our own lives, things are going to change and we will rarely be able to control these changes. Perhaps nothing is more stressful than this fact that we have so little control over what is happening to us and around us. We have been trained to believe the opposite—to think that we have a great deal of power and control over our lives and that we can assert ourselves and create the positive changes we desire. Thus we have been raised to fail! Most of our circumstances and the great majority of our lives are simply not in our control.

The Illusion of Control

Let us consider the top ten most stressful items on the Holmes and Rahe Scale: death of a spouse, divorce, marital separation, jail term, death of a close family member, personal injury or illness, marriage, fired from job, marital reconciliation, and retirement. It is fairly obvious to realize which of these we have absolutely no control over: death, injury, illness, and retirement. We know we cannot control when we or others will die or become sick or injured. We also know that at some point we are going to be too old to work and must retire. We may believe we have some control over deciding when to retire (taking early retirement, for example), but we cannot change the fact that we must stop working at some point. We may be more confused about the amount of control we exert in the situations involving divorce, separation, marriage, or reconciliation. However, when we examine the relevant facts, we can see that our choices to do these things are dependent upon others and that we do not exert complete control. We may badly want one of these to occur, but if our partner does not, it will not happen.

The stressor of serving a prison sentence may seem to be something we can control, but how much control do we have if we are wrongfully accused? And even when we are guilty, the fact of incarceration and the length of the sentence depend upon others and are not in our control at all. The last of the ten stressors, being fired from a job, may at first seem to be something we can control, unless we are caught in the all-too-familiar situation of corporate downsizing, merging, or the organization going out of business. Much of what happens to us at work depends on factors completely out of our control—the economy, cultural and political changes, personalities, and corporate needs. When we believe that we can control the degree of change affecting our lives, we are living under an illusion, and this may be the most destructive and stress-producing problem of all.

The Necessity for Stress

As mentioned, stress is generated by the positive events in life just as much as it is produced by the negative ones. Change, whether it be perceived as good or bad, produces stress. We may not consider change stressful when we are happy with the results, but the fact that change has occurred means there is stress in our lives. Items on the scale that are ambiguous and can be perceived as either positive or negative are: pregnancy, change in health of a family member, gain of a new family member, business readjustment, change in financial state, change to a different line of work, change in number of arguments with spouse, son or daughter leaving home, spouse beginning or stopping work, and change in living conditions. All of these items may be interpreted in a positive manner, but they will still be stressful.

The importance of realizing that stress can be caused by positive changes is the recognition that stress itself is not a negative part of our being. We need a certain amount of stress in order to function; we cannot act or live up to our potential in an entirely stress-free environment. Stress is not an enemy or something to fear; it is a normal part of our lives that serves to motivate, drive, and sometimes force us into expanding ourselves and doing things we otherwise would not. How many students would study a textbook without the stress of an impending exam? How many of us would go to work when we did not feel like it without the stress of fearing for our jobs? How many of us would clean our homes if we were not stressed by dirt and disorder? How many of us would pay our bills if we did not have the stress of bad credit hanging over our heads? The stressors in these cases provide the motivations for doing things we may not want to do. They also provide the opportunity of removing the stress when we do take care of them. In other words stress is necessary to prevent us from being too comfortable, overly complacent, and lazy. We do not change when we are comfortable; stress produces some pain and discomfort, which causes us to move, produce, be active, and function in those situations where, without it, we might not.

The Reality of Stress

Stress can be positive and necessary, up to a certain degree. However, once we have passed a positive limit, its productive benefits can quickly become destructive, and we may become incapacitated. This is popularly defined as being "stressed out" or "stressed to the max." While a certain amount of stress is necessary and normal to life, too much of it is unnecessary and abnormal. This condition clearly affects both the quality of our lives and our health. The relationship between stress and our most serious illnesses is a strong and conclusive one: Too much stress kills just as surely as do bullets. When we pile on the stressors and allow ourselves to live in constant, uncontrollable high stress, we are involved in slow but sure suicide. We are literally killing ourselves.

How can we reconcile the fact that we have very little control over the stressors in our lives and yet, if we allow them completely to control us, they will kill us? How can we recognize when we have crossed that invisible line that separates positive, needed stress from destructive, unnecessary stress? How can we obtain the balance for ourselves in which we have constructive stress without crossing the line into destructive stress? These are not easy questions to answer. This is evident by the fact that we are a nation of overstressed individuals manifesting a rapidly growing number of stress-related diseases. Our Doing model has placed critical emphasis on achievement, and achieving is stressful. We have been taught to fix things by taking action; we have not been trained in the concept of doing less to get more. As a culture we have not yet recognized the importance of being. We have not learned as a society how to become balanced, how to meaningfully set priorities for what is important, and how to deal with stress. Most of us tend to become stuck in old patterns and even to derive comfort from the fact that others around us seem to be as stressed as we are. We have become familiar with too much stress; we tend to resist giving up that which is familiar, even when we know it is destructive. We fear change, even though it is part of life and inescapable. We believe, as we have been trained to, that we must control change; we are unaware that this attempt to control what cannot be controlled produces great, unnecessary, and eventually deadly stress.

The Problem with Choices

Perhaps we are all allergic to making decisions. Or at the very least we all have difficulty with the big decisions, the ones with consequences that change our lives. All of us, at some time, have experienced a struggle over what choice to make, and we have faced a situation in which we made the wrong decision. Many of us, when confronted with a hard decision, know how painful and stressful this process can be; we may wish that we could avoid dealing with these difficult choices in life. At such times it is easy to forget that we are experienced and masterful decision makers and that our lives are composed of constant choices, just as much as they are made up of change.

During most of our daily activities we are not consciously aware that we are always involved in decision making. Almost everything we do, say, believe, and feel contains an element of choice. From the moment we awake until the moment we fall asleep, we make decisions that affect our day. We choose when to get up (even though we may believe the alarm clock is doing so, it is our decision to set it and obey it), what to wear, what to eat or drink, whether we talk or not, which route to drive, what errands to run, how productive we are going to be, how social we are, and so on. There is no adult activity that does not involve making a choice, be it conscious or not. But these are not the typically stressful decisions of our lives; these *are* our lives. The choices that drive us crazy and cause us to be acutely aware of the pain involved in our decision-making strategies are the ones that involve consequences and commitments. These are the decisions that we know will change our lives; these are the choices that, once made, cannot easily be changed.

The Difficulty with Decisions

The difficulty of a decision is determined by its relative importance and the relevant changes that will occur. Significant choices usually lead to significant changes. The more responsibility (power and control) we assume for the change caused by our choice, the more painful the decision-making process will be and the more stress we will incur until the decision is made. These are the times we may wish we had a crystal ball to reveal the future. We feel stressed because we cannot know right now which is the best choice for the future. And of course what makes these decisions even more painful is the possibility of being wrong, appearing stupid, or causing others to be rightfully critical of our ignorance or inability to choose well. Inherent in all major decisions is this probability of failure. For those with high self-esteem and mature confidence, this process will be difficult. For those with no self-esteem it may be impossible.

We have been trained to believe that these life-changing choices put us on the line; what we decide and how we do so are tests of our intelligence, courage, and coping styles. We have been taught that our worth, character, and strength are exposed to the world when we face the big decisions of life. Above all, we have learned to fear failure. It is no wonder that we feel stressed, pressured, and often unable to cope in these situations. There is too much at stake at these times. Or so we believe.

Most of us are not only allergic to decisions, but also afraid of risk. This fear alone will produce tension, stress, and anxiety about the decision-making process; it may lead to "risky" actions or quick, impulsive choices in order to alleviate the stress and the emotional discomfort. All major choices in life force us to confront our weak egos—we face the possibility of being wrong, losing status or, even worse, losing things we highly value and are attached to. We are afraid of making the wrong choices, changing our lives in the wrong direction, and experiencing future regrets and pain. This fear of the future is the definition of anxiety. Nothing is as paralyzing in the here and now as the fear of what may happen later. Most of us will try to actively avoid being placed in this predicament.

Avoidance of Choice

The foregoing difficulties make it easy to recognize why there are very few great decision makers in the world and why they are usually honored for being such. They help us to understand why even the best decision makers sometimes fail. When the stakes are really high, most of us would rather not play. There are many ways in which we can avoid making the big choices, but the two most common are either to delegate or to defer. We avoid the stress of the process, the responsibility for the outcome, and facing our fear of risk when we turn the decision over to someone else. This is a similar process to scapegoating, in that we make someone else responsible for our life choices. This is also the easy way to appease our weak egos and avoid the risk of making a mistake or being wrong. When we are concerned with being perfect, or appearing to be perfect, we will delegate as many of our critical choices as we can. If we cannot do so, then we may try to defer or escape from the decision-making process. The simplest method is to run away or refuse to make any decision at all. If we cannot admit that we are evading the decision, we may procrastinate making any choice as long as possible. Avoiding making any decision is also a defense against stress, even though the major stressor is not the process itself but the consequences of it. This is a passive-aggressive style of functioning, which creates a great deal of tension and stress for the decision maker as well as the others involved in the situation. It can result in poor decisions finally made as a result of stress and pressure. Impulsive decisions made by the risky decision maker and based on immediate actions also often function to alleviate emotional tension. While the end results—the impulsive decision—may look the same, the approaches utilized by the deferring and risk-taking decision makers are quite different. Any decisions made in order to reduce emotional discomfort are not going to be as good or effective as those made with careful consideration and appropriate information.

Decisions and Self-esteem

There is a very strong relationship between the decisions we make and the way we feel about ourselves. Inherent in all informed decisions are the possibility of great rewards; we feel better about who we are when we make good choices. We are also rewarded by others for our ability and intelligence when the decision pays off positively. We may also gain status when our choice leads to the consequences that others desire. Our confidence increases, our fears decrease, we feel effective and useful, and we like being the risk taker. All of this feels good and we feel good about ourselves, for the moment. Because most big decisions involve the interests and welfare of others, it is natural that we are concerned with what others think about us during the decision-making process and afterward, when our choice will be tested by time. This concern for others may be natural, but it is not the basis for real self-esteem. While it may be very difficult, it may even be impossible, to make a choice of some magnitude without considering how others may feel, we still need to resist placing our worth and value onto what others think of us or how they judge the consequences of our decisions. Otherwise when we place our esteem outside of ourselves, we are involved in the work of the weak ego.

Self-esteem always means self-approval; we look inside ourselves for our worth and value. This does not mean that we do not consider others in our decision-making process—important choices that are solely ours with no consequences for others rarely exist—but we need to be able to distinguish between the feelings of others toward us and our feelings about ourselves. In other words we cannot base our decisions upon receiving esteem and status from others (or anything external), but we need to remain true to what is right internally. We need to focus upon doing the best we can for ourselves; we need to be our own constant judge and jury. The big choices we make in life determine the path of our own lives. They shape who and what we are, what we do and how we feel about ourselves. They cannot be made to appease others or to satisfy our own weak egos. We cannot make these choices in order to get our needs met through the externals in life—status, money, fame, adulation, or social rewards.

It is possible to have it all; we can be true to ourselves first and also get the external goodies. Many decisions lead to this outcome. The ones that do not, however, are those where we must choose between self-approval according to our own internal values and other-approval based on external standards. When we turn against ourselves, we end up with nothing. All the externals in the world cannot give us what we really need. Satisfying the weak ego always means opposing our internal self. Nothing that we will ever decide or choose is worth losing our Selves. No choice that alienates us from our spirits and souls can ever be considered the "right" choice.

The Challenge

None of this is easy. The process of decision making is a difficult one, precisely because we have so little control over either the choice itself or the consequences that will occur once we make the decision. This process can become extremely painful if we are faced with the dilemma of pleasing others versus pleasing ourselves. No one enjoys being in limbo; not knowing which way to turn, feeling lost and confused, having no clear sense of direction may be the most painful experiences we can ever face. However, it is while we are in this state that we can quickly see the relationship between choices and changes. Our choices lead to our changes and our changes affect our choices. When we have problems accepting one, we will have difficulties with the other. The problems of coping with changes and decisions are the same ones; we fear what we do not know, cannot control, and are unable to predict. We fear change and we fear the choices that lead to change. Our training has compounded this fear by adding the element of responsibility to what we are unable to control. We are taught to feel responsible when we make a "bad" decision or the "wrong" choice, even though we cannot control all the variables in the process. We are also taught that we must control our lives, even though there is very little in our lives that we can actually control.

Furthermore, to make matters worse, we have been trained to consider others above ourselves, especially when it comes to the big changes and the great decisions in our lives. Very few of us have been taught to be true to ourselves; there are very few external rewards given to those who go against the mainstream of life. How many of us have made important choices on the basis of what somebody else wanted? How many of us have let someone else decide something important about our life? How many of us have "gone along" to appease, placate, or not cause trouble? We have been trained to be *nice,* but we have not been taught how to be *real.* Our society tends to reward appearances more than it does character; it tends to choose mediocrity over creativity. To paraphrase Carlos Castaneda in his Don Juan series, we have but two choices—to choose not to be a fool and to walk alone or to choose to be a fool and to walk with other fools.

The Questions

When the future changes or the decisions that need to be made seem overwhelming and we are unable to act on them, it may be helpful to ask ourselves the following three questions:

1. Is this the right decision or change that needs to be made? Often we can get caught up in a situation where we feel that something is not working or it needs to be done differently. We decide to make a change just to be doing *something.* We may be trying to force change to occur or rashly decide to take action just to alleviate the stress of the situation. We can recognize this is the case when no decision that is proposed seems to be satisfactory. This may be a situation in which we are dealing with unnecessary changes rather than confronting the reality of the problem.

2. *Is this the right time for the change or the decision?* Timing is critical in everything. If we cannot seem to make a decision, consider the timing. Does it need to be made now? Sometimes we know what the change or decision has to be, but we cannot act on it because the timing is wrong. When the timing is right, the decision process will be much easier and more natural than when the timing is off.

3. *Is the right person making the decision?* It is so easy to make decisions for others and so very difficult to make them for ourselves. It is helpful here to ask who is going to be most affected by the change, who is going to have to do the most work, and whose life is under consideration. If we are trying to make a change or choice that rightfully is not ours to make, we will be met with great resistance. We can use this resistance to examine exactly what we are doing. When we make our own decisions and allow others to do the same, the process is much smoother and simpler.

The Solution

Living life is a heroic task. Being a hero frequently means being alone. Most of the world will choose conformity over courage, appeasement over causing trouble, risk avoidance over risk taking. For most, going against the training—the Doing model—is too problematic and painful. The paradox here is that following the model creates more unnecessary problems and destructive pain than going against it does. The model is insufficient for dealing with life, but the model is easy. It presents the illusion of control, the illusion of a quick fix, and the illusion of success. Never mind that all these are illusory; the important thing is that they are powerful and seem to be achievable without a great deal of internal work. It is interesting to note that the longer we remain on the model, the more difficult it seems to be to do the internal work. The more value we place on the externals, the more foreign the internal world seems. How absurd it is that we are more afraid of our own insides than we are of this crazy external world!

Changes and choices would not be major stressors for us if we could relinquish the concept of responsibility without control. The idea of change is difficult only because we foster the illusion of being able to control it. The same holds true for the decision-making process. Once we give up our attachment to being able to control everything, we become more open to accepting that change is inevitable. If we also give up the idea that we must be perfect and accept that we will make mistakes, but we will also fix them—that our lives need mistakes in order for us to learn—then making choices becomes easier. So what if we make a mistake; we can learn from it and choose something else next time. If we recognize that we cannot be perfect, then we can also recognize that we cannot be a perfect failure.

The changes we encounter and the choices we make may remain difficult—life is not supposed to be easy—but the processes themselves will become easier if we remain true to ourselves. In order to do so, we cannot remain entrenched on the Doing model, but must spend the important parts of our lives Being. Becoming a good decision maker involves developing the same skills as those of being an effective problem solver. Both require a strong sense of the self, the knowledge that all the important characteristics are internal, and that the Self has validity and great worth. If we recognize that we are good and that this goodness is not dependent upon making the right choices or pleasing others, the process becomes much clearer. We can never be completely lost if we know who we are inside. We will never let the world totally confuse or confound us if we have a strong sense of the Self. We do not need to base our coping skills on what others are doing or thinking if we focus on what we are doing and thinking. The solution to dealing with changes and choices is exactly the same solution for all our other life stressors: Be true to the Self. To personalize this, you must know who you are and what is important to you; honor yourself and trust your own instincts; consider others only after you have taken care of yourself. Above all, you must do what feels right to you. By doing all these, you will have fewer regrets and self-recriminations and you will be being your best.

VIII ∽ Problem-Solving Changes and Choices

1. Accepting

Begin by accepting the simple facts that life is change and that it involves making choices. You cannot escape from either. Accept that you may not like them, but that they are the reality and that nothing you can ever do will stop the process of change or choice. Furthermore accept that you are powerless to control the direction of the changes or the consequences of your choices. In most cases what happens is not in your control. If this is too difficult for you, accept the fact that you may be a control addict. If so, you will need to recognize the hold that your weak ego has over you.

Self-esteem necessitates knowing and loving yourself, and part of this awareness involves the recognition of how very little control you really have over anything. Loving yourself allows you to recognize this lack of control and live with it. While recognizing the fact that control is illusory may be painful for you to deal with, it is more than compensated by the realization that you do not have to assume responsibility where there is no control. Your weak ego may crave this responsibility as a measure of your status or worth in the world, but your self-esteem realizes that you do not want or need to be so encumbered.

Accept the fact that you cannot always be right. You will make some mistakes and choose the wrong things at times. All of this is normal and natural. Do not want to always be "right"; you will learn much more of value when you are "wrong." Once you can accept this, it will be much easier to let go of your fears of choosing and deciding. If you are willing to accept the fact that you made the wrong choice, you will be more willing to take risks. Since all of life is a risk, and all your choices involve some element of uncertainty, this acceptance is a necessary precursor to being an effective decision maker.

It may be the supreme irony that the only truly critical choice you really have—whether you live or die—is the decision that you rarely deal with. And this one, the big one, is not in your hands at all. If the biggest choice of all is not yours to decide, why sweat the smaller ones? The only decision you can really control is to be the best you can, as you determine, from moment to moment. This is the one choice that is completely yours to make. How strange it is that this is the one you probably avoid much of the time. Accept that this is the important one and focus on it next time you are involved in a major change-and-choice process.

2. Letting Go

Begin with letting go of your fears—of the future, of your inability to control so much of your choices and changes, and of being wrong. This is a lot to let go of, and you have not been trained to do so. When you do let go of fear, you will soon discover that most of your problems about decision making will also be solved. When you are in a situation calling for a life-changing decision, your fear is what will paralyze you and cause you to be stuck in limbo. What you are usually most afraid of is doing something now that will have dire consequences or of acting in a way you will later regret. These are all symptoms of the fear of failure.

Another thing that makes decisions and changes so difficult is the fear of losing stature by being wrong. This is a symptom of your weak ego. In order to let go of these powerful fears, it helps to perceive your life as a learning process instead of a goal or completion. When you do this, you recognize that making mistakes, being wrong, and choosing things that do not have the desired outcomes are all part of your learning and growth, and therefore all have great value. If you can decrease the power of your weak ego by increasing the strength of your self-esteem, you will become less concerned with what others think or how they view you. This is extremely liberating and allows you to face your choices and changes cleanly and objectively.

Let go of your guilt and anxieties because, once again, they will prevent you from living in the present. Your guilt is a product of your past and you cannot change what has already happened. Decisions motivated by guilt are rarely going to produce positive effects, but usually will prolong the guilt and increase the regrets. Decisions motivated by anxiety are usually about avoidance or a desperate need to do something in order to ease the discomfort. They will also not produce beneficial results because in this case the decision-making process is being used to alleviate stressful feelings rather than to make the best choice. Anxiety relates to the future, and this is also not in your control. The only thing you can control is yourself in this moment. Let go of trying to control anything else; you will only fail.

Let go of your fear of taking risks. All of life is a risk and you have been taking them since you were born. There is a difference between constructive risks—those things that are necessary in order to live fully—and destructive risks—those things that are unnecessary and dangerous. Constructive risks are similar to informed decision making: You gather the appropriate information, deal with your emotions until you have become reasonably objective, remain true to yourself, and then make the best choice you can. In this way you are minimizing the destructiveness of the risk and maximizing the excitement of it. After all, risks are exhilarating; they are what life is all about. Without them your life would be very dull and quite meaningless.

3. Expressing Feelings

Change can be frightening; choices are often frustrating. It is normal for you to be afraid and upset about things you cannot control or predict. But there is a huge difference between feeling upset and allowing your feelings to control your actions. You will need to let go of your fears, and the best way to do so is to express them and release them before they drive you to make choices based on what you are feeling. In other words your feelings are there—you cannot control them—but they are not the major or only consideration in your decision-making strategies. It is normal to feel tension and be stressed when you are confronted by situations that call for changes or choices. It is natural to want to alleviate this type of stress, and you can do so by simply expressing what you are feeling before you actually act or choose.

There is time between the feeling and the behavior. Use this time to acknowledge your emotions; in this way you will be remaining true to yourself and accepting the reality of who you are, as your feelings are a critical component of your reality. But they are not the only component. Honor them, for they are there and they are a necessary part of you. Once you have done so, you can then go on to a more objective perspective. If you are angry, sad, confused, scared, stressed, nervous, or whatever, admit it. Talk about whatever you are feeling, to yourself, to trusted others, to a therapist. Let all your feelings about the situation surface; do not try to repress or rationalize during this step.

Remember, your feelings only require acknowledgment; they do not need action in order to be released. Once you have dealt honestly with what you are feeling, then you can go on to the mental or philosophical states. It is okay that you hate change and are afraid of doing the wrong thing. It is normal to be uncomfortable when confronted with change. It is natural to want to return to a safe place. By expressing yourself, you will avoid becoming paralyzed or ineffective. You will avoid remaining in unnecessary limbo, and the time you spend on this step will result in less time spent on the actual change process.

4. Taking Responsibility

This is a critical step when dealing with changes and choices because many of your problems associated with these stressors occur when you try to delegate or escape from choices that are rightfully yours to make. Begin this step by recognizing that it is your life you are dealing with and that you are the only person totally responsible for your own life. Once you became an adult, you became responsible for yourself. You are totally responsible for anything that you can completely control. You are partially responsible for whatever part is in your control. Life changes and important choices are never completely in your control, as there are so many unknown factors and external variables separate from you.

When there is so very little that you do actually control, it seems a shame to try to delegate or escape from what you can. Be clean with yourself. Take responsibility for the things that are yours, for the decisions that are critical for your own life, for the changes that are part of you. If you allow others to decide for you or to face the consequences that you avoided by delegation or evasion, take responsibility for your inaction and do not blame them for what has happened to you. Remember the old saying: "If you do not vote, you cannot complain." It is your life—make sure you vote on whatever you can. If you make the right choice, congratulate yourself. If you make the wrong one, admit it, learn from it, change it, and go on. When you think about it, there really is no "wrong" choice if you learn something from everything that happens to you.

Think of your life as a process, and honor your mistakes and "bad" decisions as teachers along the way. It is ridiculous to regret anything that has taught you, changed you, and helped you to become what you now are. Avoid regrets and recriminations by taking responsibility and doing the best you can. Do not lose or waste your precious life being afraid of what is going to happen or being obsessed by what has already happened. There is no way you can be alive and not take risks. Be true to yourself, and the risks will be worthwhile. Take responsibility for what is yours, let others do the same, and you will discover that changes and choices are not problems but the fabric of your complete life.

5. Forgiving

Forgive yourself for not always knowing what you need to do or what is the "right" thing to do. Nobody has all this information. Forgive yourself for being wrong; everybody has failed at something. Allow yourself to be human—imperfect and fallible—and forgive yourself for not always remembering this. Remember, you are much more than what you have been taught to believe. Your spirit and soul are not keeping score on whether you are right or wrong, winning or losing. Perhaps your soul thrives on the mistakes of your life because your successes often feed your weak ego and create the need for external power and esteem from others. These are not the attributes of the soul. When you are humbled, when you are confused, when you are admitting your imperfections and failures, your soul is nurtured. Paradoxically, you become closer to God when you are vulnerable and uncertain than when you feel confident and comfortable.

You do not have to forgive yourself for your vulnerability, as this is a direct link to your spirituality. You may need to forgive yourself when you feel justified, when you have "won," when the world gives you status and worth, as these are the links to the weak ego. You can do a good job, make the correct choices, and be soulful as long as you do not get caught up in your external worth. Anything of lasting value for you is internal. Forgive yourself when you forget this or choose not to act on it. Forgive others for doing the same. This is very difficult, but you can do it. The process becomes easier the longer you practice it; you will become internally stronger each time you are able to forgive.

6. Appreciating

Appreciate the fact that all of life is risky and that your risks make your life interesting and worthwhile. Realize that everything changes and that this prevents you from becoming extremely bored. Appreciate that you will always be making decisions and that your life is composed of millions of choices. You will always be changing, you will always be choosing, and doing so means that you are alive. Once you can move beyond the fear and stress of the change and choice processes, you will see the excitement inherent in it all. When you positively look forward to something, you are eagerly anticipating it. When you negatively dread an occurrence, you are anxious. Anxiety and anticipation are very similar—something is going to happen and it is out of your control. The difference between them is in the emotions you feel at the moment. When you can let go of your fear and accept your lack of control, you will have many more anticipatory moments and fewer anxious ones in your life.

You can control the way you feel about changes and choices. Recognize that they are inevitable and prepare to deal with whatever happens. You are a skilled risk taker; you are becoming a masterful problem solver; everything that will happen to you in the future is a challenge. Appreciate that you have many challenges ahead of you and also appreciate that you will cope. You can do it, you will do it, you are always going to be the best you can be for yourself. Appreciate that this is what living life to the fullest means.

7. Rewarding

And now for the fun step. Reward yourself for all the hard work you have already done. Reward yourself for recognizing that you have changed a great deal already in your life, you are changing right now, and you will continue to change. Recognize where you are in this process and reward yourself for being here. Think back on all the major decisions you have already made and reward yourself, if you haven't already done so, for all of them, the "good" and the "bad" ones, the ones that worked and the ones that failed. At least you confronted and made those decisions rather than putting them off. Yes, reward yourself for the ones you have always regretted, because they taught you a great deal and caused you to change.

Try to perceive the positive in all the choices you have made, because there is always something good to be found. Exchange any past regrets for rewards so that you can continue regret-free instead of regret-ful. It is quite easy to be confronted with a difficult decision, spend all your energy on trying to evaluate its consequences, and then later punish yourself for making the wrong choice. In other words it is normal to forget the difficulty involved in the actual decision-making process when you are only concerned with unknown future results. Take some time to remember the process and give yourself a reward for doing something that was quite difficult.

All your efforts and hard work deserve rewarding, and you are the only one who knows how much you have invested in getting you where you are now. Reward yourself for all your efforts and give yourself what you most need. You have been taught to wait for the world to reward you. And if the world does not, which is usually the case, you feel slighted or over-looked. Change this now by giving yourself what you hoped you would get when you were doing the hard work. Give your-self that pat on your back, that praise, that emotional lift. Give yourself a psychological "raise." Tell yourself you did a good job, your effort is appreciated, your worth is great, and you are loved and cared about. You are, you know!

From envy, hatred, and malice,
and all uncharitableness,
Good Lord, deliver us.

—Book of Common Prayer

IX ↝ *Beliefs and Biases*

We have been trained to value what we believe and rarely to consider or question how these beliefs developed. Moreover we are also taught how to think and feel about what we believe; we feel justified in upholding the creeds and doctrines that govern our lives and even, if necessary, dying for them. Thus what we think we are is determined, to a large degree, by what we hold dear; our chosen values and convictions become some of the most important aspects of our lives. We are defined, labeled, and accepted or rejected depending upon what we believe; our belonging to a particular society is largely dependent upon some adherence to that culture's value systems. The Western model, this society, our country, institutions, personal principles, and mores are all based upon some choice of doctrine; this choice is often radically different from what others have selected and chosen to live by. The choices of belief systems are numerous and varied, but what we as humans all share is the intensity of feeling and the need to believe in something.

All religions, politics, governments, and organizational and educational groups are founded upon some chosen value system that defines and structures the attitudes and behavior of its participants. The problems with these systems begin when we forget that they are by necessity limited and restrictive, and we act as if they are truths or absolutes rather than one of a number of possible choices. Difficulties intensify when we believe that what we are espousing is the only good or "right" way to think or act. These problems multiply when we try to impose our beliefs upon others or when we become destructively critical of other systems. When we judge others negatively for holding different beliefs, we become biased and prejudiced. When we act hatefully because of these differences, we become bigots.

Demands and Conflicts

Just as it is a human trait to feel and value intensely whatever it is that we believe, so it is also human to become passionately attached to our opinions and to want to share them with others. This need to share quickly progresses into the need to convince others and to gain their approval and agreement. If we succeed in this, there is a further progression into requiring their validation as further justification for our belief. And once we require something, it does not take very much time until we expect or demand others to comply. It is no wonder that discussions about belief systems frequently become major conflicts between family members, social groups, and eventually even entire countries. Thus what began as a difference of opinion has escalated into war. To some degree all of us tend to repeat this process throughout our lives. We continue to create problems for ourselves when we demand agreement and conformity from others. And yet this is a very difficult lesson for us to learn. There are very few positive outcomes to arguments about different beliefs. At the very least we will feel uncomfortable when engaged in emotional disagreements, and our discomfort can quickly lead to overreactions and becoming out of control. These situations can lead to humiliation, and there is always the possibility that we will hurt or destroy relationships and drive people away from us, even though we really do love and value these disagreeing ones. In the worst case these conflicts can result in killing or being killed by those who believe differently. What is this great need we have to share our views and to passionately convince others to believe our convictions? How did we become so intolerant and demanding?

Humans everywhere seem to be passionate about their religions, countries (patriotism), families, sports, and food. We all depend upon family and nurturance for physical survival; we need religion for spiritual development, country and home for connection, and a sense of belonging and sports for recreation and entertainment. We are familiar with what we know, and what we know is what we have been raised with. After all, the word *familiar* originally meant "having to do with family." We are threatened by what is unfamiliar and different. It is always easier to demand change from others than it is to attempt it ourselves. To be open to what is different, to be tolerant of what is strange, and to be accepting of the unfamiliar requires great security and inner strength. Unfortunately this is not what is learned from the world, but rather what we must develop from what we learn about ourselves.

The Reality About Belief Systems

Many of the concepts Americans hold dear and fight to preserve are derived from our Western belief system. Our ways of behaving, thinking, and feeling are to a large extent shaped by the Doing model. All models, including this one, are superficial and therefore limited frameworks, guides, patterns, or maps that help us to construct a manageable concept of reality. Models themselves cannot be the reality of what they are depicting, but only a representation of some part of that reality. They function to provide a way for us to perceive the world in an organized, meaningful manner. They can help us understand some part of the whole and they provide a means for dealing with what we are perceiving. We may come to believe that our perceptions are reality, but they can only ever be an exemplification of a small part of reality at a particular time and place. Thus the models we choose and the insights we develop can never encompass all that is real, but can only reflect our awareness and familiarity with a chosen paradigm or piece of reality.

As abstract as all this may sound, it is important to be able to differentiate between: (a) reality—that which is real; (b) models that represent a way of depicting reality—our paradigms or guides; (c) the perceptions we hold—our insights, intuitions, and awareness; and (d) the feelings we have toward ourselves and others. The interrelationship between all four is the reason that belief systems can so easily lead to conflicts. If we can separate and distinguish between these diverse things, then we can begin to accept that belief systems, because they are derived from models, cannot and need not be universally similar. Our strong needs to be validated and understood combined with our desires to belong often cause us to demand that others share our belief and value systems. However, this is an unrealistic and impossible goal.

Cultural Conditioning

We define ourselves by what we believe and trust; we often forget that we have learned these concepts from a cultural model and that others have learned different standards. We receive consensual validation—agreement and approval—from those around us, who have also learned from the same model. Our beliefs and opinions are reinforced and strengthened when others agree with us. Because America is a large country and many of the immigrants who come here adopt its creeds and values, it is understandable that many of us believe we have the best or the most acceptable belief system of all. All humans are conditioned by their cultures to believe that what they do, how they think, and what they feel is the most appropriate action or response. All of us have been rewarded for being culturally appropriate; we are understood, reinforced, and made to feel that we belong. We have also been punished by criticism or prejudice when we have gone against our cultural training.

For example patriotism has always been a valued belief, leading to the conviction that we must defend our country when asked to do so. During the Vietnam war those who refused to serve or deserted were punished by the nation and labeled as outcasts. Interestingly those who served were not rewarded in the ways typical of past wars and conflicts, indicating that a cultural change was about to occur. As a result the idea of defending the country whenever politicians decide it is necessary has become more controversial. We still consider patriotism a valued trait, but we are culturally more open to questioning "patriotic" decisions made by others.

Differences Between Models

The Western model teaches us that being individualistic is preferable to being collective. Americans learn to be oriented to the individual rather than to the group. We also believe that achieving the task or goal is more important than developing relationships, so we tend to place less emphasis on relating and more on accomplishing. The Doing model is a masculine one, meaning that it exemplifies and reinforces assertive, tough, goal-driven, and overt styles of behavior. This is in contrast to cultures with feminine models, which value modesty, tenderness, quality-of-life issues, and sensitivity. The Western model teaches us to deal directly, to value open communications, and to confront when necessary. Therefore we are less skilled with being flexible or with understanding nonverbal or nondirect communications than are those cultures that place more value on indirect skills.

The Doing model has a universal focus, meaning that the rules are made for all with few exceptions. Truth in this culture is considered absolute. Other cultures practice more exceptions to the rules based on relationships and believe that truth is flexible depending on who, what, and where. We are taught to believe that the future is in our control and is the most important of the three time dimensions. Many others believe that the future is determined by fate and is therefore the least important dimension. Likewise this culture believes that it can (and should) control nature; this is in opposition to those who believe that we must find harmony and balance with nature. The Doing model teaches us that success is determined by material possessions; other models believe that success involves spiritual growth. The Western concept of thought is that it needs to be rational; other cultures believe it needs to be intuitive.

Just as we have learned our belief system from our culture, so also we have been taught what to honor and value; these teachings create our biases. This culture is partial to: quantity (more money, more things) versus quality (fewer but better); competition (we want to win) versus cooperation (helping the group succeed); risk takers (the successful rebels, the confronters, the individual spirit) versus face savers (the pacifists, the socially skilled, and the conformers). We value mobility (progress and action) over continuity (history and tradition) and we most clearly are biased toward youth over maturity. None of these choices are wrong; they may not even be conscious choices that we have made. Just as our hormones determine our sex, so does our culture determine our beliefs and reinforce our choices. We simply cannot exist without believing in something and having certain biases. This is our human legacy.

Personalizing the Model

Now, how does all of this relate to you? If you grew up under the Western model, can you now conceive of not wanting individual recognition because this cannot include the entire group? Can you imagine being embarrassed for winning or successfully accomplishing a task because this has resulted in you being singled out of the group? If you had the choice between working with others and getting no individual recognition but instead having the entire group rewarded versus working alone and getting a personal reward, which would you choose? Could you cheat, not for yourself, but to help a friend do better than you did on a test? Could you defer your own needs or wants to those of the group even though the group has different needs than you? Can you imagine being flexible (changeable) with your constructs about truth, what is right, and what is acceptable? Can you conceive of feeling ashamed because you expressed your own opinions? All of these behaviors are derived from belief systems in other cultures and they are all practiced and valued in other societies today. Can you now see how much you have been conditioned to act and feel and to value what you believe by your culturally determined belief system?

The Difficulties Emerge

Problems do not occur because we believe or have certain prejudices. They occur when we want others to believe and feel as we do. When we try to force others to change their beliefs and accept ours, we create conflict. Our beliefs and biases become directly related to our insecurities when we try to convince others to believe as we do in order for us to be comfortable or reassured. When we are not secure, different belief systems threaten us and cause us to feel uncertain or unsafe. Converting others by forcing them to change is a sign of insecurity and not a mark of strength, but this is not what the Western model has taught us. We have been taught, rather, to equate strength with certainty and with might. Our culture has trained us to spread the word and to convert the world. When others do agree with our beliefs, we have consensual validation, but this agreement does not mean that our beliefs or values are right or that we have discovered *the answers*. This holds true even with our most important doctrines. Every religion is based upon a belief system. Likewise democracy, socialism, or any other political doctrine is based on a value system. Our culture prides itself on having religious and political freedom, yet we are remarkably intolerant of different systems. In reality America reinforces the Christian ethic, the democratic system, and an orientation to the individual. We give lip service to the concept of acceptance, but we generally mistrust those who believe differently. This lack of acceptance is a cultural phenomenon that needs to be questioned by each of us. When we become truly secure within ourselves, it will become easier for us to accept and allow differences among others.

The Problem with Choice

Belief systems cannot be totally laissez-faire. We simply cannot exist without feeling strongly about certain things. Because our culture is not a fatalistic one, it would be impossible for most of us to understand not intervening with fate, or in other words completely accepting any situation. There are cultures, however, that do this; they believe that all actions are predetermined and that fate is responsible for whatever happens in life. Because all belief systems imply choice, it would be impossible for any of us to try to encompass all of them. We exist, we believe, and we choose what is important to us. This is not the problem. Others do the same. Again this is not the problem. The problem is that we cannot always live in peace with those who oppose us. Evil does exist in this world; others do hold opinions and prejudices that are dangerous to us. Others choose to be hateful or hurtful and to practice evil. Accepting their right to do so will be impossible if we are victimized by them. Thus we cannot avoid having problems.

Even when we are very secure in our own beliefs and try not to inflict them upon anyone else, we are going to be confronted and challenged when someone tries to inflict his or her beliefs upon us. The ideal of living and letting live is unrealistic when others deliberately try to hurt or harm us or those we love. Therefore it is somewhat simplistic to state that we should all believe what we choose and let others do the same. As long as there are those who believe that life is without meaning, that property is worth more than life, and that what they want is more important than the harm it may cause to another, belief systems, biases, and choices are going to provide continual problems for us to resolve.

The Problem of Freedom

One of the most problematic of cultural beliefs concerns government. Our concept of democracy is founded upon the essential freedoms of the person; this creates the cultural bias of the importance of the individual. We in America value the right to express ourselves, to bear arms, to practice our personal preferences, and to feel relatively free to do what we want. Because this belief system respects the rights of each person, we have developed a political and legal system that protects the individual, even when detrimental to the society. These personal freedoms have resulted in overwhelming crime problems and a judicial system that often protects the criminal at the expense of the victim. Collective cultures, on the other hand, restrict the rights of the individual and support the good of the group. In these societies individuals do not have as many personal freedoms, but they do have more freedom from crime and from being victimized. Thus freedom becomes relative and somewhat abstract. Under our system freedom for the individual results in the society suffering. Under other systems freedom for the society results in the individual being restricted. Proponents of both systems will always be in conflict, and both sides have justification for the merit of each. Both sides can also agree that their system is flawed.

The Problem of Religion

History has shown us that more wars are fought in the name of God than for any other reason. At this very moment horrible atrocities are being committed due to religious differences. In spite of the remarkable similarities that exist between all religious doctrines, and in the face of common teachings concerning peace, love, brotherhood, and understanding that are at the foundation of all major religions, humans continue to hate and hurt and even kill those who believe a different doctrine. It is ironic that the path to salvation is so bloody. Religious beliefs may well be the best case analysis of trying to force others to think exactly as we do. Perhaps this is because religion involves our deepest insecurities—our own worth and goodness. If we do not know that we are good and have great worth, it is easy to become threatened by others. If we think our worth depends on believing a certain creed, if we define our goodness—our relationship with God—by how we define God rather than how we define our Selves, then it is understandable why we cannot tolerate other possibilities. It then becomes easy to act upon our biases and to project our insecurities onto those who define God differently than we do.

The weak ego tells us that we must be special. Just as the small child wants to be the one chosen by his parent, so do we want to be the special ones to God, our ultimate parent. The insecure child will act out, demand attention, exhibit noisy and even destructive behavior when attention is withheld, and lash out against others as a projection of his or her own pain from being ignored or feeling unloved. At the heart of all oppression lies this same kind of fundamental insecurity. If we are insecure, it is much easier to justify ourselves by blaming others than it is to work on becoming secure. As we become more secure, we discover that our needs to have others agree by believing or behaving as we do lessens. Just as the parent functions to give the child a sense of worth and to educate him (or her) about life, so also does God function to give us the awareness of our own goodness and to provide the lessons we need to learn. When we rebel against these lessons, no matter what our age, we create unnecessary problems that cause pain to the ones we are rebelling against and, even worse, hurt and destroy ourselves. And when we are in pain, it is very easy to inflict this pain upon others. Ultimately we are at war with our Self; in this war, God becomes another innocent victim of our insecurities.

The Problem with Principles

When we hold beliefs that are really important to us and that define who we are and how we act, we call these beliefs principles. Our principles become the ultimate sources of our belief systems and function as motivating forces and fundamental truths. Because they are such critical components of our being, we become passionate and emotional about them. These are the concepts that we hold most dear and that cause us to feel most threatened when challenged. Rarely do we remember that they reflect our personal choices and that these choices are somewhat biased. Principles are essential personal beliefs; for this reason we need to be careful not to inflict them upon others. Many of our unnecessary problems can be avoided by following this simple rule: The more involved and emotional we are with a principle, the more careful we need to be about forcing it upon others. Everyone else has the same right to feel as emotional about his or her principles as we do about ours. No one else needs to adopt our belief systems in order to validate us. This is one area in life where two rights frequently lead to wrong.

The very nature of a principle implies that it contains some truth, defines some right, and therefore becomes something basic and critical for perceiving ourselves and guiding our actions. Our foundations are composed of many principles; such choices cause each of us to be unique. When we become secure and develop solid, constructive foundations, we discover that agreement with others is not necessary. It may be nice and it may be more comfortable when others do agree with us, but it is not critical to our Being. We also realize that others cannot build our foundations. Their principles are an intrinsic part of themselves and not building blocks for us to use. So it is with our principles—they are our own blocks, and no one else has to use or agree or even accept them. It may help if we can think of our principles as precious jewels: just as we would not throw our jewels around and insist that others take them and wear them, so also we can honor our principles. We can learn to keep them close to our hearts, keep them out of our mouths, and value them as our own personal and private treasures.

X ❧ Problem-Solving Beliefs and Biases

1. Accepting

Accepting the rights of others and tolerating their differences will be impossible if you have not yet accepted yourself. If you have any doubts about where your insecurities lie or hide, a passionate conversation about religion, politics, individual rights, abortion, or the criminal system with someone who opposes you will bring them out in full force. These conversations can be entertaining and even enlightening when the participants are secure about themselves (secure is not the same as sure!), but they can result in unnecessary, destructive, and aggressive confrontations when the parties are insecure and intolerant of one another's rights. It can be very difficult to be tolerant of conflicting opinions when you are engaged in passionate debates or face-to-face conflicts. When you are engaged in a heated defense, it is extremely difficult to remember that what you believe at this time is different from what you once believed. You have changed and you will continue to change; your opponent will also change, but it is not your task to decide the direction of the change. As long as you and your opponent are enjoying a heated debate and know how to control the outcome, there is no problem. But as soon as the disagreement becomes uncontrollable or fatal (begins to hurt the relationship), your difficulties have begun. If you get to the point where you feel out of control, if you blame your aggressive or hurtful behavior on the other, or if you act in ways you will later regret, you have gone too far. And if you make negative judgments or harsh criticisms about others simply because they believe differently than you, you have become less than your best. You are demonstrating your insecurities and giving in to your weak ego.

It is not always important to win by convincing others that you are right and they are wrong, or misinformed. You can hold wonderful beliefs—truth, justice, fairness, love, and peace—but if you act destructively while trying to project or force them upon others, you are not being wonderful. You are not practicing what you are professing to believe. It is important to accept that you will not always be right and that even when you are, you may act wrongly. If you can be wrong, so can some of your beliefs be wrong—at least for others. Winning by coercing others to accept that you are right and they are wrong is not the task of your life; this does nothing to help you learn. What you believe is not as critical as how you behave. Accepting begins when you can truly live and practice the concept that you do not know everything and that others can disagree with you. When you allow others to believe as they choose, express their opinions, and feel that they are right, especially when you "know" they are "wrong," you become accepting. And when you can actually listen to an opponent with open ears and a flexible, tolerant mind, you become wise. Acceptance is critical; without it you will remain intolerant, just one of the many who use positive beliefs to justify negative deeds.

2. Letting Go

One of the main reasons you may have difficulty accepting or tolerating differing beliefs is that you are unsure of your own foundation, your own sense of worth. You may wonder what will be left of you if you stop espousing or defending what you believe. The answer is you only need to know one belief about yourself—the awareness that you are good—to be complete. You can let go of all the others and still function well. If you know this one, then none of your other values and principles need be rigid or constant. Letting go is not as difficult when you remember all the things that you once believed and no longer do. History is composed of belief systems that have been challenged and changed. It was once heresy to believe that the earth revolved around the sun, that the world was not flat, or that life could be controlled by man rather than by God. Technology and science have expanded the possibilities and changed the ideas that were once considered immutable. Now we know the world is round, planets revolve around the sun, time is flexible, and that science can to some degree control life. In the future what we now believe to be real or right may be expanded or drastically changed, causing our present convictions to seem limited and perhaps even ridiculous.

You cannot let go of believing; you can let go of your attachment to what you believe. You believe because you are human; you attach to what you believe in order to feel secure and make sense of your world. The more you need to cling to your concepts for managing the world, the more dependent you will be on receiving validation and agreement from others. Thus your attachments become your chains, reinforce your biases, and foster intolerance. What began as a choice has become a need and created a dependency. Let go of your insecurities and you will find you are also letting go of your prejudices. Let go of your needs for others to agree and you will find that you are more tolerant. Let go of your weak ego—your need for esteem from others—and you will discover the worth inside yourself and also inside everyone else. Change your focus from what you believe to how you behave. Stop questioning what others may believe and instead question why you feel the need to convince them that you are right. This need is your attachment and this you can change. Learn that the more secure you become, the less you will need to defend yourself. Let go of your defensiveness, let go of your judgments of others, and let go of negative or destructive criticisms. These actually reflect your insecurities and lack of faith in yourself. When you let go of your attachments, you truly become free. Your strength lies in the way you feel about yourself and not in the conviction that you are right. Be strong. Let go!

3. Expressing Feelings

As you have worked through the previous steps, you have probably discovered a great number of feelings. You may be angry that your right to defend your beliefs is being questioned. You may have been trained to try to convert others to your religion, government, or personal rights. You may believe that an important part of your life needs to be dedicated to "saving others" from themselves or from erroneous belief systems. You may be feeling sad and somewhat confused because your fundamental beliefs are being threatened. If so, recognize that your training is causing these problems. Express your feelings, whatever they may be, before you do anything else. Let your anger and frustration, your sorrow and confusion, out. Do this in a safe environment, one in which you will be supported rather than opposed. What you feel is not to be criticized or questioned; your feelings are yours and you cannot control them. Do not try to do so.

One of the biggest problems you may have is separating your emotions from your beliefs. Believing something and feeling it passionately may seem to be the same, but they are two different things. You can believe anything intensely and still learn to discuss it unemotionally if you can distinguish between your feelings and thoughts. It is easier to be accepted, no matter what you may believe, if you can stay calm, collected, and rational. The only way to do so is to deal with your feelings yourself rather than forcing others to deal with them when you are being overwhelmed by them. Practice being angry by yourself. Say anything you want when you are alone. Yell, scream, curse, punch your pillow, write an angry letter and then tear it into little pieces. Your anger needs to be released; this does not require an audience. The same holds true for all your feelings. Believe as you choose, feel what you feel, but try not to inflict either upon others. Your problems will diminish, you will be stronger, and your world will become a better place—a kinder, softer, more considerate, and safer environment.

4. Taking Responsibility

In order to be responsible for your own beliefs and biases, you must first become consciously aware of what you think and feel. Becoming aware may sound simple and fairly obvious, but it is really quite difficult. This is because so much of what you believe has been programmed into you from your family, teachers, culture, and the Doing model and has not been scrutinized by your own Self. Your general tendency, consistent with most humans, is probably to question the beliefs of others much more often than to reflect upon your own. Reverse this. Practice questioning what you believe, think, and feel before you become involved in an emotional discussion. Ask yourself why you think the way you do—is it based on your own experiences and awareness, or are you espousing something you grew up hearing? Where did your ideas come from? Do they "work" for you—in other words are they relevant to you at this time? Does this opinion that you are protecting and defending fit into a balanced, cohesive system for your life? Is your behavior consistent with your convictions? If you preach peace and fairness but act aggressively and with bias toward others, how meaningful are your spoken ideals? Finally, ask yourself if you like who you are based on what you believe? Are you comfortable with yourself when you share your ideas? Are you trying to communicate, or are you trying to coerce? If the answer is the latter, recognize that this is a learned style and refocus on what is causing your insecurities and what you can do to change.

If all the above sounds like a great deal of work, it is; this explains why it is more usual to find people criticizing the belief systems of others than to see them examining their own. It is easier to be externally critical than it is to be introspective. Know that criticism and judgment lead to alienation and separation. You can change this for yourself if you are willing to take responsibility for your ideals and principles. This will mean choosing not to argue about your differences with others unless you really believe that it is important and can be constructive. If your goal is to change someone else, don't do it. If your goal is to learn something or to help you question your own thinking, do it carefully. Let your opponents know that you are respectful of their opinions and that you are investigating your own. As long as you can remain rational and calm, you can debate. Make the simple rule that once you become overemotional or aggressive, you will stop the discussion. In this way you will be actively taking responsibility for yourself and you will avoid many unnecessary problems associated with your beliefs and biases. Remember that highly emotional discussions are rarely productive and that uncontrolled outbursts are often destructive. Try to avoid heated debates, as they generally cause problems without resolutions and they create more dissension than they cure.

5. Forgiving

The need to forgive yourself for your beliefs and biases may at first seem abstract and rather unnecessary. However, when you recognize that much of your behavior develops from your thoughts and feelings, the need to forgive becomes clear. Since all forgiveness implies blame, you can only forgive yourself for what you can control and then take responsibility for. Everything that you believe may not be in your control, just as your thoughts and feelings are not always in your control. But you can control your actions—the ways in which you express your beliefs and cope with your biases. These are the areas that may require forgiveness. It is not always easy to distinguish exactly what is your part, because it is in your control, from what is not yours and not in your control. You may be forced to act upon a belief that is not yours, such as defending your country or your organization or even your family, when your personal opinions may be in opposition to your behavior. There are many instances in which you do not have complete choice or control of what you do or even what you say. You will have to determine how much responsibility is yours; this is the part that you can forgive, if need be. You cannot blame yourself and then forgive yourself for anything that is not in your control. Likewise you cannot absolve yourself of responsibility and refuse to take the blame for what is in your power. If this is unclear, ask yourself realistically what you could have done differently. If there were other choices you could have made, and you chose wrongly, use this information. Take the responsibility and then forgive yourself so that you can get on with the business of living. Forgiveness is a positive, constructive choice; regrets and recriminations are the opposite, destructive choices. Everything, including all your choices, are part of your personal learning process. You learn better choices from making the wrong ones; it is really that simple. Choose well next time. Forgive yourself for your mistakes, for inflicting your beliefs upon others, for acting in a prejudiced way, for not being perfect, for not always knowing right from wrong, and for not being sensitive and kind enough. Forgive yourself for the past and resolve to change, to be better, to try something else. That is the best you can ever do. And it is enough!

Once you forgive yourself, it is easier to do the same with others. There will be some things that seem past forgiveness—there are atrocities, evil acts, and unspeakable horrors going on all the time. These may seem impossible to forgive. You can learn to forgive even when you do not understand; you can forgive even when you will never forget. You forgive others because it frees you. The inability to forgive keeps you imprisoned; not forgiving does not hurt the other nearly as much as it does you. For this reason forgiveness is a critical problem-solving step. Get professional help if you cannot do it on your own. You will never understand the reasons for the pain in this world. Know that understanding is not the task of your life. Your task in life is to be the best you can be to and for yourself;

this becomes impossible when you are weighed down with hate, anger, and prejudice. You will not be able to be charitable when you are consumed with revenge. Do not carry the negativity of the world; your soul cannot deal with such a weight. Forgive yourself in order to be better; forgive others in order to be free.

6. Appreciating

Recognize that your beliefs and principles have given you a foundation, a sense of yourself that you can build upon. Know also that your biases have given you a sense of safety and a connection with others. You can appreciate that much of your intelligence is defined by your ability to believe and your choice of opinions. You can also be grateful that some of these choices allow you to belong within your society and help you to communicate within your culture. Without beliefs and principles you would have very limited conversations and very little to share with others. Now appreciate that there is still much to learn outside your present awareness. Thank God that you have the ability and the potential to learn. Be grateful for your conscience, for it is your guide in helping you to make good choices. It alerts you to your mistakes and makes you aware when you need to change. Appreciate the fact that you feel uncomfortable at times, and this is often your conscience letting you know that you are in dangerous territory.

There is something to appreciate about all belief systems; there are always similarities to be found. If the ideas themselves are diametrically opposed to yours, look at the feelings and the expression of the beliefs. The intensity may be similar to your own. Your opponent may reveal a need for security that may remind you of your own needs. When you find the similarities between humans, systems, and expressions, you will be able to appreciate them. Yes, the differences also exist, but finding differences is easy and not rewarding. This will keep you involved in the superficial. When you scratch beneath the surface and go beyond the externals, you will find similarities. Appreciate that these are what unite you with others and give you great joy. Appreciating what is different and unfamiliar will not limit or constrict you, but instead will enlarge and expand your vision and awareness. And this is a definition of growth and wisdom.

Finally, appreciate your sense of humor, for it allows you to laugh at yourself—your idiosyncrasies, your mistakes, and your insecurities. You will recognize that you have learned, matured, and become wise when you begin to laugh at your own seriousness. What was once so important, perhaps even tragically so, can often be looked back on as extremely amusing. Some of your worst dilemmas and most awful mistakes later become your funniest stories. Be thankful that you can laugh at yourself and with others. Your life does not always have to be intense and serious. When you laugh, you are free. Having a sense of humor is one of the most precious gifts you possess.

7. Rewarding

Give yourself a reward for getting to this step. By being here you have demonstrated your openness and taken a risk to try something new and different. This discussion about beliefs and biases is a difficult one; it has forced you to confront your training, your weak ego and insecurities, and your resistance to change. You deserve a reward for persevering; give yourself one. You have probably been taught that you are what you believe and that being right is very important. Now you are learning that you are more than what you believe and that being right is not the most important thing in life. Whenever you go against your training, you are doing hard work and you deserve to be rewarded for your efforts. Give yourself internal rewards—be proud of yourself, be nice to you, pay yourself compliments, acknowledge your own worth. When you do so, you will discover that you need fewer external rewards.

Self-esteem needs en-couragement: you will need to give yourself courage when you are doing something new and unfamiliar. Rewarding yourself is one of the most encouraging tasks you can do. As with all things, practice makes it easier. Practice rewarding yourself throughout your day. Reward yourself every time you question your own beliefs rather than judging others. When you listen instead of debate, reward yourself. If you are able to remain calm in what would previously have been a heated confrontation, give yourself a big reward. Recognize how difficult this is and then do something nice for yourself. Self-esteem is about loving yourself *and* treating yourself in a loving way. Rewarding yourself is one of the most loving ways you can manifest your own self-esteem. After you have rewarded yourself, you can reward others. This is easy, as you have been trained to take care of others and you know exactly how to reward them. The hard task is feeling worthy of rewarding yourself. You are learning, changing, and growing and this may be one of your greatest rewards.

XI ⁓ Disease and Disorders

Most of us think of disease as illness or sickness, which is the modern concept, but it is the earlier definition of *disease* as "discomfort or lack of ease" that more clearly describes our problems with it. All dis-ease can be conceptualized as a lack of comfort with the Self, be it emotional, physical, mental, or spiritual. Actually it is difficult to separate disease into a specific category, as our discomforts affect and reflect the totality of the Self. When one part suffers, the whole suffers. This focus on the whole person—holistic treatment—is becoming more common due to the realization that the medical model, with its focus on only the diseased section, is incomplete. Actually the concept of treating all aspects of a person is an ancient one, which was generally disregarded when science and technology became the foundations of modern medicine. The recent trends toward treating the complete person and combining modern technology with old remedies make good sense, but are still not widely accepted.

The Holistic View

People are complex, and yet there is a surprising simplicity at the core of all of us. When we are well, we manifest balance, harmony, and connectedness throughout the totality of ourselves. When we are sick, we are not at ease and therefore are alienated from some aspect of ourselves. The traditional medical model focuses on a specific area for treatment and generally tends to ignore all other aspects of the person. However, it is simplistic to compartmentalize disease and treatment to only one part of our being; eventually all parts suffer and need treating. A simple example of this is the common cold: We focus on and treat the physical symptoms (runny nose, sore throat, watery eyes, coughing, aching) but tend to forget the effects on our mental abilities (fuzzy, slow, and inaccurate processing abilities), our emotional states (feeling depressed and vulnerable), and our spiritual sides (feeling different, alone, and unconnected). And when the disease increases in severity, all the symptoms intensify. From a systems perspective, which means looking at the whole, all this makes perfect sense. Why is it, then, that we are surprised and frequently shocked by the effects of disease on what we consider unrelated parts of ourselves? Why do we keep on trying to compartmentalize illness into neat categories and refer to it either as mental illness, emotional disorders, physical ailments, or spiritual unrest? Why do we continue to want to isolate in order to treat?

The Mechanistic View

The answers, once again, are found in our training from the Doing model. We are taught to think sequentially and in a linear fashion in order to solve our problems. Thus if one part of us is sick, we are trained to separate it from the whole and treat it without relation to the other, supposedly healthy sides. The assumption is that we can then fix what is wrong and that the whole will function as before. This is a mechanistic view and one that does not really work with humans. We are not machines; our souls, emotions, and mental abilities are not visible; and treatment is rarely simple. Yet the traditional medical establishment, based on concepts from our linear Western model, continues to function as if we were machines. Some examples of this are the following: when our hearts are bad, we replace them; when we have cancer, we excise it; and when we have any serious illness, we think in terms of medicating, removing, replacing when possible, and restoring.

None of this is wrong or problematic *if* we do it at the same time that we take into consideration all parts of the total person. Unfortunately this is not usually the case. Most often we consider traditional medical solutions to be the complete process, and we fail to consider the source or cause of the disease, or its effect upon the whole being. Then we wonder why the treatment often "fails." The concepts of success or failure also come from our dichotomous training and frequently result in overly simplistic assessments of outcome. The cancer has been removed; therefore the treatment is successful. It is no matter that the patient feels depressed, mentally incapable, and spiritually dead; medically the outcome is considered positive. One more machine has been fixed.

The Medical Model

Our traditional medical model is not a bad one; it is just an incomplete one. It is based on the following assumptions:

1. Disease is unnatural (and therefore "bad")
2. When something is broken, fix it quickly
3. If it cannot be fixed, it is no longer of interest
4. When it is not "fixable," there is often a sense of personal failure by the adherents of this model (the doctors and the patients)
5. Alternative treatments are suspect and discouraged

These assumptions come directly from the Doing model and result in the same limitations and potentials for difficulty encountered in our other problem areas. Because the model is competitive and goal oriented, and values external manifestations of success, there should be no surprise that many medical professionals also exhibit these traits and foster the concept of supreme authority (expertise).

In the past, and presently to some degree, society reinforced the idea that doctors are reflections of our patriarchial concept of God—not to be questioned. When we are diseased, we desire some ultimate authority to heal us. We turn our complete selves over to an authority, even though these experts have been trained to specialize only in some specific and limited capacity. Perhaps when we are ill, we become similar to little children: We long for the perfect parent to take care of us and fix our problem. Traditional health care has developed and reinforced the views that healers cure and that treatment and responsibility rest in the hands of professionals. Therefore the person who best knows the total system, the person who is suffering, is not usually consulted during the treatment process. We have learned to abdicate the responsibility for our well-being. We have not been taught to be equal partners with our physicians regarding our health care. Thus we are all responsible for this lopsided system; we are all culpable when it fails.

The Importance of a Process Concept

How do we begin to change this long-established idea of medical might and right? How do we become more involved in the treatment process and work toward becoming self-healing? We know we cannot change the system, so we need to focus on what we can change. A good beginning to these answers may be for us to learn to conceive of disease as process rather than a state of being. We have been taught to view disease as negative, as something "bad" and somehow separate from us. Our reliance on expertise has reinforced the notions that we are helpless in the face of illness and dependent upon professional experts to "fix" us. This vulnerability is a further reflection of the highly-desired-but-impossible-to-obtain quest for a life that is easy and comfortable, requires little effort, and produces complete satisfaction and happiness. In other words we yearn to be taken care of and we become lazy in the caretaking process. Perhaps laziness is a malignancy of the soul, just as cancer is a malignancy of the body. If we use a process-oriented perspective, dis-ease may be one means of ending the laziness by producing the possibility for change and growth. What we do and how we feel about ourselves when we are diseased can lead to positive (benign) or negative (malignant) outcomes.

We know that personal change does not occur when we are comfortable and satisfied. It comes when we are miserable, struggling, frustrated, and willing to take risks and try new possibilities. All illness (dis-comfort, dis-ease, dis-order) can then be considered a catalyst for change, a possibility for internal growth, and a means of becoming unattached. Perhaps it can also be considered a manifestation of overattachment to some part of ourselves, a part that needs to be worked on. All of this does not mean that we have complete control over our diseases or that we always bring them upon ourselves. We are not responsible for what we cannot control and therefore we cannot always be blamed for the lack of complete control over our disorders. We do not always cause our diseases, but maybe we do require them as vehicles for change. If so, then we need to understand how the process of disease, rather than the state of being sick, can work for us instead of against us.

We cognitively know that we will get sick. At some level we are aware that illness is a natural state of being. It is unnatural to live an entire lifetime without disorders, dysfunctions, and diseases. The completely and truly healthy human is a rarity.

And yet we forget all these facts when we become ill. It would be extremely difficult, if not impossible, to welcome our disorders or to like our dysfunctions. (If we do, we exhibit another form of illness!) Fortunately, it is part of the human condition to want to be well, to strive toward health. From this comes our ability to rejuvenate, recuperate, and grow. Our diseases, similar to our other problems, give us possibilities to stretch, expand, enhance, and learn. The wounding of one of our parts may lead to the healing of another. For example a physical illness may create a spiritual wellness or new emotional awareness. This phenomenon is often seen among those who are critically ill. This does not mean that we want to be unwell. It does mean, however, that when we are unhealthy, we can evaluate the process—the learning—even though we do not enjoy the state—being dis-eased.

Rethinking Disease

The Self is sick and the illness first manifests itself in one aspect of the whole. Because our training has taught us to regard disease as unnatural, we will usually try to deny (by ignoring), or defend (by overcompensating), or dismiss (by medicating) what is "wrong" with us. When this does not work, we search for the quickest fix, usually by consulting an expert. Our medical model aids and abets us when it can. In those cases where there is not a simple remedy, we despair. Rarely do we begin by questioning the cause of our dysfunction. We have not learned to approach our disease by asking what it is trying to tell us or teach us, and how it can help us. We have not been trained to look upon our disorders as warnings or guides to learning about our Selves. We have not been taught to think of symptoms as signals and signs along our life path. Instead we have been programmed to believe that we must be perfect, our bodies must work at all times, and sickness is a sign of weakness and failure. It is no wonder, then, that we become fearful, resentful, and frustrated; disease, according to our training, is a manifestation of imperfection. And this, we have learned, is not acceptable.

Once we have questioned the cause of our illness, the next step in the process is to discover what we are being taught. How is this sickness working *for* us? (We already know how it is working against us, right?) What lesson are we supposed to learn from it? Perhaps the answer is as simple as just to slow down and do less. This is a common answer to many stress-related problems, but one that is rarely heeded. Perhaps it will mean we need to make significant life changes and refocus our energies. Or it may lead us to spend more time working on ourselves. Whatever the answer, if we can recognize that our ailments are telling us something and pointing the way toward new possibilities, we will learn from them. Hating our disabilities, fighting against them—which means fighting ourselves, as the disease is part of us—refusing to accept that there is a necessary lesson, and going against the natural process will not lead us toward integration and health, but will only prolong our painful journey. Recovery does not always mean going back to our previous condition; recovery often means acceptance of the new state we have reached. Yes, it is a painful process (life means pain), but it can be a productive one.

The Fear of Disease

All of the foregoing will still not remove the initial horror and fear we experience when we learn that we are sick. It would not be normal to welcome illness without being afraid of it. These feelings of terror are part of the natural process and they are not quickly or easily removed by considerations of what is good about the disease or of how we could have prevented it. Acting as if we do not care or being gallant about the illness is a denial of the reality of the situation. The awareness that this is all a natural process does not come quickly, unless it is superficial. Likewise a preoccupation with the cause and nature of the dysfunction is another way of avoiding the reality. This kind of involvement with the how and why of an illness can become an obsession that prevents us from learning and growing.

The hows and whys may be interesting from an abstract perspective, but they do not ease the pain or remove the fear. They may explain mentally what is occurring, but they do not help us deal with our problem emotionally. All too often they impede our emotional process and progress by focusing on the mental aspect of trying to understand the illness rationally. This can be a distancing mechanism and a way to escape dealing with the pain. These defenses also block our spiritual learning by keeping us grounded in explanations. Above all, these preoccupations allow us to compartmentalize our disorders in order to treat them, instead of searching for the interrelationships between the diseased part and the totality of our Selves.

Treating the Whole

Treatment of all disease needs to be based on the interrelationship of parts to the whole. We can separate the whole into parts in order to select the preferable treatment modality, as long as we do not forget that all our aspects also need to be treated. In other words if our disease manifests physically, we would probably turn to the medical establishment first. Then we may also consider getting help with our emotional problems. We also need support, empathy, and acceptance from others. Closeting ourselves away from the world while we try to heal would not be good treatment. Family, friends, and professional help are there for us, and we need to ask for their help. We do not need to feel ashamed, or as if we have failed in some way. These negative feelings will only feed our illness. In the same manner we need help with our mental side. Much of what we are thinking comes directly from our training. The Doing model is not the one of choice when we are sick. This is an excellent time to change models and practice Being. The popular notions that you are responsible for your sickness, that you have caused it, and that your disease is just retribution for your behavior reflect society's sickness. We do not have to take on this unnecessary additional sickness when we are already ill. We also do not have to burden ourselves with traditional religious beliefs that our diseases are our punishments for being "bad." This type of negativity is unnecessary, unwelcome, and destructive to the important business of getting better, of healing our Selves.

Medical doctors try to heal the body, psychologists and counselors try to heal the emotions and mental problems, educational experts try to heal learning difficulties, and religious authorities try to heal the spirit and soul. It is shocking how infrequently these "experts" talk among themselves and relate with one another. Most holistic practitioners try to deal with the whole person, but because they are outside the traditional models of treatment, they are often untrained and unqualified. As yet there is no system for integrating all these experts in order to provide easy access for the sick patient. Instead there seems to be intense competition over clients and a general lack of respect for those skills outside the expert's domain. This lack of communication between healers frequently results in dire consequences for the patient who is trying to treat all aspects of the whole. It is easy to become confused, frustrated, and even more ill when dealing with conflicting advice. When suggested treatments are not compatible, as is usually the case, the patient suffers. It is impossible to do everything, to try all suggested cures, to become eased among so much contradiction. It is easier, then, to pick one expert and ignore all the others. So patients choose orthodox treatments, or therapy, or prayers, or alternative medications and risk missing complete treatment. This does not occur due to lack of information, of not caring or trying, but rather when there are too much information, too many theories, too many opposing healers. At the moment this is the current state of affairs, although there is a growing trend toward meaningful integration.

The mind-body connection has recently become popular, due to best-selling books, media attention, and the popularity of alternative treatments. This is essentially an integration between Eastern therapies (meditation, prevention, holistic diagnoses) and Western technology and skill. The Eastern model is concerned with the mind and the cognitive processes, which can prevent or alleviate our disorders. The Western model involves the physiological aspect of the illness. In tandem this combination is believed to maintain good health, prevent disease from occurring, and minimize negative effects when disease is present. This type of integration is important and welcome, as long as the emotional and spiritual sides of the person are also considered. The fact that maintenance and prevention are becoming important factors in the medical model are positive steps in the direction of treating the whole.

The Positive Environment

There are other factors besides integration that can dramatically impact the treatment process. A major one is the patient's support system. Recent research indicates that supportive environmental conditions for the patient can have amazing positive results. Compared with being alone and not receiving support, having others who care and are nurturing can work "miracles." Studies consistently show that it is important to feel loved, to belong, and to have positive help when we are sick.

We recover faster, the effects of the disease are minimized, and we tend to learn and grow in a constructive direction when we allow others to share and be with us in our illness. Just the opposite occurs when we alienate ourselves—our disease rapidly progresses, we lose our sense of belongingness and connection, and we may even die earlier than necessary.

Even when we do not have a strong human support system, we can achieve great benefit from other living things. Animals have been found to have great therapeutic value; some hospitals and nursing homes are allowing patients to have pets or to have animals visit with them. The results of such experiments have been dramatic, and the difference between having such exposure or not is clear. When we are diseased, we need more loving contact, not less. We need something to touch and hold and love, even more than we normally do. Touch is a critically essential part of our lives. Infants who are taken care of physically but who lack tactile stimulation will die. Similarly patients who do not have something to touch and hold do not heal as quickly as those who do, and they may even die earlier as a result of the lack of tactile contact. Even plants can have therapeutic effects. There is a positive relationship that exists between all life-forms; watching something grow, being around life, and being in life are critical to living.

The Negative Environment

A social support system is clearly positive; a codependent relationship when we are ill is negative. The problem occurs when we cannot recognize the difference between these two. In order to recognize negative dynamics, we must understand that using our illness for secondary gains is part of a destructive, sick pattern. Secondary gains are defined as manipulations: trying to have all our needs met by others; using our illness to get love, approval, sympathy, control, or attention; or wanting to stay sick because the benefits from being so outweigh those of being well. The codependent in this system is the caretaker, or the "well" person, who is sacrificing himself to the patient. Thus the patient's health becomes more important than the well-being of the caretaker. Often this system appears externally positive because we have been trained to take care of others at the expense of ourselves. We have been programmed to believe that we must put the needs of others above our own; when the other is sick, we must take good care of him or her, no matter what the personal cost to ourself. This sounds altruistic and positive, but more often than not this type of thinking produces two or more sick people—the identified patient and the caretaker, who can readily become emotionally and even physically ill.

All this does not mean that we cannot be there for those we love when they are ill. This is a time when we are going to put aside some of our own needs and desires in order to help the patient. We are going to want to do this to some degree. This issue of degree is the key to determining when and how much we caretake. If we have no regard for the Self, and no consideration about our own health and needs, we are apt to give too much and become emotionally needy and physically drained. We can only effectively give the gift of ourselves to someone else for short periods of time or for time that is clearly bounded. When someone we love is dying, we know that our caretaking has an end. When someone is recovering, we know that he or she will need us less and less each day. The paradox here is that too much caretaking, or a heavy dependence on the other, can prolong the illness and be detrimental to the patient, as well as to the nurturer. No sick person needs another sick person taking care of him or her; two sick people cannot provide a conducive environment to health. The healthy environment means that there is balance and functioning between individuals and that there is an allowance for change. As the patient progresses, the caretaker recognizes and reinforces the change process. This is part of the reason why the support system can be therapeutic and constructive for both the patient and the caretaker. No one involved needs the sickness to define his or her role; neither is being abusive to the other or to their Selves.

The Influence of Emotions

Medical studies and research on the family have clearly demonstrated that there is a genetic predisposition to many of our disorders. Illnesses tend to run in families. We also know that the relationship between emotional styles in the family and the predisposition to types of disease is also strong. In other words if cancer is common within a family and the family's style is to suppress anger, then a member of this family will have two strong vulnerabilities toward contracting cancer, one learned (nurture) and one inherited (nature). Genetic engineering is not yet advanced enough to prevent or remove our flawed genes (this day will come!), but we can minimize the risks by changing our emotional behavior. Being well balanced, getting rid of anger constructively, treating depression effectively, and lowering stress levels will certainly minimize the possibility of cancer or any other predisposed illness. At the very least, working on emotional well-being will intensify and hasten the recovery process. Denying or ignoring the emotional aspect will do the opposite and prolong or inhibit the treatment process.

Suppose, however, that our disease or disorder is causing the emotional problems. We are physically ill, and this is what is making us angry, depressed, and stressed. We considered ourselves emotionally stable until we became sick, but now we are off balance. Here the attribution of cause is not the important consideration. We can only control two things completely: how we feel about ourselves (our choice to love or hate ourselves) and how we manifest these feelings (our behavior based on our feelings). Nothing else, including the disease, is in our total control. When we choose to love ourselves as flawed, imperfect beings, and to treat ourselves as if we are worthy of being loved, we may not cure our disorder, but we will be doing the very best we can in our diseased condition. Certainly we will not be making ourselves more sick than we need to be.

Blaming emotional disturbance upon physical ailments may feel natural or normal, but what we are actually doing is exacerbating the problem. Of course we are not expected to feel wonderful because we are ill, and there are times we are going to be unhappy due to our condition, but there is a balance that can be achieved. Our emotions will run the gamut, as they usually do, and they may feel more intensified when we are sick, but there will be times when we feel positive, happy, and at peace. Clinging only to negative emotions is self-destructive and unnecessary.

Recognizing the Emotional Connection

A large body of research confirms that our emotions have a great deal to do with our disorders. We have known for some time that depression is highly correlated with cancer. What we do not know is the cause-and-effect procedure: Does depression predispose us to cancer or does the cancer cause the depression? Whatever the relationship, it clearly exists; we recognize that both our emotional and our physical conditions are clearly affected. We also know that stress, defined by a combination of physical, psychological, and emotional reactions, can lead to many physical disorders, ranging from mild dysfunctions (headaches, inability to think clearly, panic attacks, ulcers) to severe disorders (arthritis, heart attacks, high blood pressure, strokes, and some types of cancer). Stress not only predisposes us to these disorders but also aggravates and prolongs the efficacy of treatment. Recently research has shown a clear connection between anger and many of our most serious diseases. The fact that this connection is logical and makes perfect sense—that what we intensely feel has an effect on our bodies—does not mean that treatment processes routinely deal with our emotional states. Traditionally they do not. Unreleased anger and unresolved issues have nowhere to go but to turn against the physical body. Anger, stress, and depression are clearly signs of disease; that they then cause disease should come as no revelation.

Flight, Fight, or Resolve

The classic stress model, or what we do when we are frustrated, may function as a good example of our emotional reactions and the options we have when we are suffering. Our first reaction may be to run away or deny what is happening. This is the famous flight response and is the natural early occurrence whenever animals or humans are confronted, afraid, stressed, or frustrated. But when we continue to deny the reality of our condition, or refuse to accept the severity of our illness, when we withdraw physically or emotionally, and when we become apathetic or stop caring about anything, we are engaged in a prolonged flight response. This may seem to be a normal human reaction, but in actuality it is a destructive and dangerous one when it becomes the primary coping style. The denial reaction is a buffer against shock and a useful defense mechanism at the beginning of painful news; it serves as an emotional and sometimes even a physical anesthetic until we are able to cope with the pain. After the initial shock has worn off and we become better able to cope, there is no longer any need for this response. Running away from a problem never works to resolve it; in this case what we are trying to escape from is within ourselves and what we are actually doing is prolonging the painful state, which precedes accepting and coping with the illness.

The second option we have is to become aggressive—the fight response. This again can be demonstrated either physically or psychologically. We can direct our aggression externally—at other people or situations that we feel are to blame—or internally toward our Self or our diseased part. Again this may be a healthy, normal response for a brief period of time, but prolonged aggressiveness increases and intensifies the negative aspects of any problem, including disease. Blaming others, fighting, trying to hurt either ourselves or others, and remaining angry and upset only add to our discomfort and actually aggravate and even prolong our sickness. Because it is easier to feel angry than it is to be sad, this is a frequent response to diseases and disorders.

The third option is the only one that is constructive and beneficial. It is also the most difficult. This response means that we cope with the disease by allowing ourselves to go through all the stages and by accepting the changes within us that are occurring. It means that we first accept and then try to resolve our denial, anger, and frustration and that we recognize our learning and growing as a result of our pain. We are problem-solving to the best of our abilities, even though we recognize that in the case of disease, our problem may not have a solution and that we may not be "fixed." When this is true, our emphasis needs to be on the growth and development process. It is a human trait to be emotional, but it is also human to be rational and to develop effective coping strategies. Our usual pattern when dealing with trauma is first to respond emotionally and then to move to the rational. Disease does not provide an exception to this pattern; rather it responds beautifully to problem-solving options. We may not be able to cure our problem, but we most certainly can enhance ourselves by learning from the process.

The Self-esteem Intervention

Developing self-esteem (loving and acting lovingly toward the self) is not a guarantee against nor a cure for life's disorders. It is not the quick fix or the path to happiness. But it is the only way that makes sense in terms of living up to our fullest potential, and it will help us separate the necessary from the unnecessary disorders of life. It is amazing that few of us would consider kicking a sick dog or an ill child, but how readily we kick ourselves (emotionally, mentally, spiritually, and sometimes literally) when we are ill. This is the time to be more loving, more understanding, more caring, but we have not been trained to think this way. Retraining ourselves when we are ill may be more difficult than learning something new when we are well. It may be more difficult, but it is not impossible. This may even be one of the main reasons for the illness—to provide the desperation and discomfort necessary in order to risk the change.

When we are diseased, we are willing to try anything to get better. We appreciate our health in a different and more intense manner than when we are healthy. Becoming sick teaches us to prioritize the important things in our lives very quickly. It teaches us perspective and shows us what is meaningful. We begin to appreciate what we have and what we have lost. We quickly see where our real life meaning lies, and we are better able to cut through inessential and unnecessary distractors. When we are not diseased, it is easier to become lost in the mundane and unimportant factors of living. Thus our illness may be a gift from God, as all these gifts contain the possibility for something awful and wonderful at the same time.

Having self-esteem involves both process and content. The acquisition of it is the process, and this is a lifelong task. Learning to love ourselves and behave lovingly toward ourselves and toward others reinforces loving ourselves, because we truly like ourselves better when we are kind and caring to others. This is not something that we can do once, in order to feel esteemed. This is a continuous and frequently difficult process, which requires a strong commitment to our own worth and goodness. Self-esteem is also content because what we do when we are esteeming ourselves, how we act and behave, and ultimately how we feel, are all an inseparable part of our Selves and our lives. Our behavior becomes who we are; our feelings that guide this behavior are also who we are. There is no clear boundary between the process and the content of self-esteem. However, the boundary between having it and lacking it is extremely clear.

Emotional Illness

Many emotional disorders begin with this basic lack of self-worth or unawareness of our own identity. "Who am I?" becomes an impossible question for an emotionally disordered person. In order to answer it, this person will often construct an elaborate facade with which to fool the world. Frequently the appearance of esteem and worth will be shown, even though the foundation for these positive attributes is lacking. In other words many emotionally disturbed people appear to be the opposite of what they feel or think about themselves. They act or project qualities that they themselves sense are false or missing. They are not only deceiving others but most often themselves. This tactic may be considered part of the flight response, because all the energy is directed not at changing or solving the deficit but at pretending or denying that it exists.

All personality disorders share a dissatisfaction with or denial of how self-behavior impacts upon others and an inability to function effectively across all domains. At the core of all known (diagnosable) personality disorders lies basic insecurity—a lack of awareness of and, by extension, trust in the underlying self. This general insecurity with the self pervades all aspects of the person and manifests physically, mentally, emotionally, and spiritually. There is a strong tendency toward using physical illness for secondary gains. Mental processing is often distorted, for these disturbed individuals tend to lose sight of reality, often in order to protect the facade they have elaborately constructed. Disturbances of mood, especially anxiety and depression, are common. Spiritually these sufferers are lost and can manifest evil, due to their evasion of responsibility and need to project blame onto others. All these disorders occur because the foundation, their true identity, is unknown to them. Not to know who one is is so terrifying that the emotionally disordered individual will go to great expense to prevent the world from discovering this terrible secret.

Types of Personality Disorders

Personality disorders have been separated by mental health practitioners into three groups for diagnostic purposes. One group appears odd or eccentric; it includes paranoid and schizoid disorders. Another group, which includes narcissistic, borderline, histrionic, and antisocial personalities, appears to be emotional, dramatic, and erratic. The third group appears anxious and fretful, and this includes avoidant, passive-aggressive, compulsive, and dependent types. None of these disorders are psychotic or "crazy" in the usual sense of the words, as there is some effective functioning in the world, although such emotionally ill people seem to have increased vulnerability toward becoming psychotic under great pressure or stress. This usually occurs when the facade is under threat. It is important to understand that the facade has replaced the foundation in determining their identities and that they have spent their lives constructing and protecting this false front.

There is a great deal of confusion between a basically healthy person and an emotionally disturbed individual who manifests an excellent facade. It is quite easy to be conned into believing that a strong facade is a sign of emotional health. Part of this confusion comes from our training. The Doing model values appearance above reality and rewards strength (even if it is artificial or inappropriate) above weakness. Our training has also taught us that being in any way selfish is wrong, but it has not distinguished between selfishness and self-centeredness. As a result we usually confuse the two and label the narcissistic or ego-centered person as selfish. In actuality what is being manifested is pure self-centeredness. Being self-centered means putting oneself in the middle of others, believing that one is more important than anyone else, and therefore more deserving of attention, praise, and esteem *from others*. This individual truly feels that he is more worthy than anyone else, but he cannot give that worth to himself. He must depend on others for his esteem. Being selfish literally means to take care of oneself—to value the Self—and this is what the self-centered individual cannot do.

The Reality of Being Selfish

One of the biggest problems in the process of learning self-esteem is that the world tells us that we cannot be selfish, and yet we must take care of the Self in order to esteem it. We have to learn to take care of our own needs, to love and be loving toward our Self, or we cannot have real worth. Our training tells us this is wrong, when in fact our training is wrong. It can be very difficult to begin the process when we are afraid of becoming selfish, with all its negative connotations. Understanding the paradox here will help solve this problem. The person who tells us how great he is, how wonderful and better than others, is the one who lacks self-esteem and needs to get his esteem from others. The person who has self-esteem knows it and does not need others to confirm it. The person who demands to have his needs met and believes he deserves this is demonstrating the weak ego, the facade. In contrast the person who is self-ish, taking care of his own needs and placing no demands on others, is demonstrating self-worth and revealing a strong identity, the foundation. The fear of becoming egoistic or narcissistic stops many from learning self-esteem. This fear is unfounded and a result of faulty training. Paradoxically when we develop self-esteem, we become sure and secure, less needy and therefore more interested in others, instead of only in ourselves. The weak ego demands all attention from others; self-esteem, by attending to the Self, needs very little external attention.

Unfortunately our culture is a narcissistic one, putting great emphasis on the "me" and teaching competition, pride, and comparison with others as the norm. The development of self-generated esteem causes individuals actually to become quite humble. They have no need for arrogance or convincing others of their value. Because their own needs have already been met, and they feel secure and worthwhile, their interest in others is open, genuine, and truly caring. Reaching out toward others and wanting to care and share with them (social interest) is a natural extension of the self-esteem process. We do not need to be taught to be loving toward others; when we are loving toward ourselves, when we feel good about who we are, we share ourselves and our goodness without thinking about it. We do these positive things because we want to and because we feel better when we are loving. Caring behavior, then, becomes part of a positive-reinforcement circle, and the process of loving ourselves becomes easier and easier. Our emotions stabilize, our mental capacities increase because we have less stress and tension to interfere, our bodies become healthier, and our spirits soar. Perhaps the development of self-esteem is the magic we are all searching for to help us be happier, healthier, and to enable us to live our lives to their fullest potential.

The Lesson

Support means giving courage; when we are ill, we need more encouragement than ever to help us stay focused on the important things in our lives. The most important of all is to love the Self, to recognize the goodness within, and to act lovingly toward the whole of our Being. Disease and disorders are great challenges for all of us; they cause us to focus on our fears, our weaknesses, and our mortality. But they can also be blessings in disguise, as they frequently provide the catalysts for our biggest changes and greatest leaps into new discoveries. Without them it would be easy to become complacent, bored, and to take life for granted. They are a reality of life and they are necessary because they keep us aware of how precious and fragile this thing called life really is. They teach us humility (always a valuable lesson), vulnerability, and empathy. Because of them we are more loving toward others, more aware of how limited and brief our lifetimes are, and more appreciative of what we have. Finally, they teach us to let go, to become unattached, and to cope with the pain of having to do so. They help us break our facades and build our foundations. They allow us to move past our fears and focus on the task of being in the moment, being real, and being loving. Disease and disorder teach us a great deal, and painful as these lessons may be, we need them.

XII ∽ Problem-Solving Disease and Disorders

1. Accepting

Acceptance of the reality and consequences of disease can be a difficult, time-consuming process. As mentioned, it is normal to avoid the actual reality of a disease at the beginning, when being diagnosed, either by denial or by elaborate defenses. This emotional anesthesia usually wears off rather quickly, as soon as the initial shock of discovery has abated. Beginning the acceptance process as quickly as possible is critical, not only for the outcome of the disease but also for the effect on the whole being and the learning process over its duration. You cannot realize your full potential, in any circumstances, unless you are honestly and completely aware of what you are dealing with. In the case of disease you are dealing with yourself. This is not happening to someone else; it is happening to you. Some part of you—your body, your mind, your feelings, or your soul—is in trouble, and ignoring this difficulty will not cause it to go away. When a part of you is diseased, the whole of you is affected. In most cases the longer you ignore something, the worse it becomes. Your diseases are like small children: They want your full attention and they act up until they get it. Pretending, denying, evading, or ignoring illness will result in alienation from your Self. This is too high a price to pay in order to try to maintain some illusion of health, or the way it used to be.

No matter how afraid you are, recognition of your fear will not kill you. However, acting irresponsibly may well kill you. Responsibility here is defined as looking at, acknowledging, and accepting what is happening to you. Once you can do this, you can proceed along the next steps toward coping, learning, and growing. The inability to accept keeps you stuck and results in putting your energy into your facade rather than upon the true foundation of your Self. One of the most effective ways of remaining stuck is to get caught in the "Why me?" question. Most likely there is not now or ever will be a definitive answer to this question. These two simple words will immediately throw you into the weak ego. By dwelling on them you will begin to judge, compare, and envy others who are not diseased. Then you will become frustrated, unnecessarily angry, and perhaps even mean and bitter.

The only good answer to "Why me?" is "Why not me?" As soon as you ask the latter, you immediately fall into the province of self-esteem. Your answers to this will place you on the path of self-awareness and new knowledge. This does not mean that you will not experience pain, and perhaps the emotional pain of your vulnerability will exceed the physical pain of your disease. You will come face-to-face with your weaknesses, your fallibility, your imperfection. This is where loving yourself becomes critical. It is much easier to love the Self when it is healthy and strong, but it is more important to love the diseased self. When you are ill, you can no longer pretend that you are perfect or whole or complete. When you accept these truths, you are no longer feeding the weak ego, which derives its esteem from the facade, from impressing others. Your acceptance of your diseased self means that you are acknowledging your humanity. You will be opening the door to discovering all aspects of your whole Self, because when one part is weak, another part grows strong in order to compensate. The honest awareness of your condition, and the recognition of the reality of its consequences, will change you. You can no longer be what you have been before. This is positive, so long as you allow it to happen. Change leads to growth, and growth is life. Your disease will cause you to investigate your life, the reality of yourself, and the things that are truly important.

2. Letting Go

When you become ill, many things need to be abandoned. This is an excellent time for assessing your meaningful priorities. It is often easier to let go of things when you are sick than when you feel healthy. The very fact that you are now weak causes your illusions and expectations, your myths and crazy training, also to weaken. You no longer have the energy to sustain the facade. You do not have the strength to appear perfect. All of this is desirable if you allow your disease to teach you what to let go of. You know you are imperfect, you know you are weak and vulnerable, and you know that you are unhappy and afraid. Let go of the idea that any of this is bad or wrong or unnatural. Let go of your misguided training and allow others to see you in your present state. You do not have to pretend to be better than you really are, not when you are well and certainly not when you are unwell. If you are afraid of letting others see you when you are down, recognize that this fear is founded on your weak ego. Let it go. No one else is perfect, either, and this idea of perfection is detrimental to all of us.

Let go of any idea that you are being punished or to blame for everything that is happening to you. You are just not that powerful and you simply do not have that much control. Bad things do happen to good people, life is not fair, and your illness is not about fairness or retribution. Since you are already experiencing pain, do not add the unnecessary and destructive pain of feeling guilt or seeking revenge. Stop hating your ill health, because you are only hating yourself. This is not a good time to punish yourself needlessly. In order not to do this, you may have to let go of the idea, learned from our sick model, that it is unnatural to be ill. Sickness is a natural phenomenon. All living things experience disease. You can only maintain health and try to prevent illness up to a point. You are human, not a machine. You are complicated, and treating you is not always simple. Let go of the idea of the quick fix.

Also let go of the illusion that you should have control over what is happening to you. You have no control over your genes, which have predisposed you to certain illnesses. You have no control over the environment, which can prove toxic in many forms. You have no control over other people and their contagious infections. You have no control over human error, and you have no control over your past, including previous mistakes. If you have so little control, how can you be responsible for your present state?

Let go of anything that makes you feel worse than you need to feel. This includes excessive anger at others or at yourself. It also includes letting go of the need to externalize your condition by blaming others, or to negatively internalize by blaming yourself. Finally, let go of making life even more difficult than it has to be. In other words be kinder to yourself than usual, and allow others to be kind, concerned, caring, and helpful to you. Let go of being stoical, but do not let go of being considerate. In other words treat yourself kindly and try not to abuse the kindnesses from others. At the same time, give yourself more of what you need and let others also give to you. You deserve it, especially when you are unwell.

3. Expressing Feelings

This most likely will not be a difficult step to do when you are suffering from an illness or disorder. Feelings come frequently and naturally when you are vulnerable. You may even feel that your floodgates have opened and will never close again. The more feelings you have repressed, the greater now the deluge. When you are in pain, you actually become more human, for you learn empathy from pain. It teaches you to relate to others on a feeling level. No one else will know exactly what you are feeling, but they will know how to share the feeling. It is natural to feel afraid when you learn that you are sick. You are normal if you are fearful of what is happening to you, because you are changing, and change is difficult and scary. It means you are entering the realm of something new and unknown. Express your fears in order to let them go. Trying to repress fear only creates more. Letting it out results in the ability to move past the fear into something more constructive. Not releasing it causes you to be stuck. Remember that courage is defined by feeling afraid and still acting, in spite of the fear. Whenever you act without fear, you are not demonstrating true courage.

When you become weak and vulnerable, you will initially become angry. This is also natural, because you have lost something you want—your health, your strength, your energy. Expressing your anger in the early stages of a disease is a healthy response. Repressing your anger, or allowing it to dominate you, is not constructive. However, you cannot begin the healing process if you are continually in a state of anger. It works as a defense against emotional pain, but only in the early stages of your new awareness. Anger quickly stops working for you and actually turns against you when you cannot express it and release it. Recognize that it is easier to be angry than to be sad or afraid. Again this reflects your training, which condones aggressive behavior and punishes so-called weak emotions.

Know that underneath all anger resides sadness. This is an important part of the process of learning and growing, but it can easily become destructive if it is repressed, or contained, or allowed to turn into depression. Sadness can be defined as the feeling of emotional pain caused by loss or by becoming unattached. You will be sad anytime you are forced to let go of something or someone you love. It reflects your caring for what you are losing. This is different from depression, which can be defined as emotional emptiness combined with cognitive states of helplessness and hopelessness. Depression may be the ultimate weapon of the weak ego, for when you are in this destructive state, you are unable to care about anyone, including yourself, or anything, including your health and life. It reflects an annihilation of the Self.

Expressing feelings constructively does not always require an audience. Crying, yelling, shaking, and trembling can be solo activities. When the feelings are very deep, due to long-term repression and denial, you may want to spend a great deal of time alone letting them out. When you are afraid of what you are feeling, ask for support and companionship with someone you trust, someone who is empathetic and truly caring of you. This may be a good time to get professional help, especially if you do not have a strong support system. Allow yourself to be held, to be supported and comforted, but do not let your confidant stop your flow of feelings. Ask him to allow you to cry or yell or shake or talk until you feel empty and drained. Expressing feelings can be an exhausting process, but it is also a cleansing one. It is important for you to cry your tears, yell your anger, tremble with your fear, and talk about what is happening to you. If you do not, you will hinder your recovery by carrying around unnecessary emotional garbage. Because you are already involved in change, and your life is not in your complete control, you may as well take advantage of your condition by cleansing and rejuvenating your emotional self.

4. Taking Responsibility

It has been mentioned that you have little control over the cause and reality of your disease, but this does not mean that you have no control over any part of it. You can only take responsibility for what you can control, which means that in the healing process you have responsibility for the totality of yourself. You would be foolish to turn yourself completely over to an expert healer and not take an active role in your illness. You may have been trained to do just this, but once again what you have been trained to do is not in your own best interests. Your disease is now part of you, and you have responsibility for how it affects the whole. No expert, no group of healers, is going to know precisely what is going on with all of you. You are the only one who knows what you need and when you need it. You are responsible for taking care of your own needs, even if this means turning to others for help with them. However, do not expect your medical doctor, the physiological expert, to take care of your emotional needs or spiritual desires. Likewise do not expect that anyone else will understand or anticipate how your disease is impacting your entirety. Get as much help as you need, and take care of your own needs when you can. You deserve to heal, to be out of pain, to shorten the duration of your illness. Taking responsibility means avoiding its unnecessary and possibly destructive aspects.

By taking responsibility for what you can do to heal yourself, you will help avoid the codependent trap. You really do not need someone to care more about your health and healing than you yourself do. If you allow this to occur, you will prolong your sickness and become even more dependent. This will lead to resentment, destructive manipulations, and the creation of a sick environment. These things will then work against the healing process and may even contribute to an unhealthy system that precludes the possibility of positive growth and change. You are the one who will learn from your disease; you are the one who can use it productively. You can only do these things when you are taking responsibility for your life, your health, and your whole self. When you give this responsibility away, you are allowing yourself to fragment and closing the possibilities for anything positive to happen. This is too big a price to pay. A good rule to follow here is do as much as you can for yourself, as long as you are not hurting yourself or prolonging your illness, and then let others help with what you cannot do. Try to avoid becoming too dependent on anyone else, and especially resist those who foster this type of dependency. Helping someone has a different connotation, and a cleaner feeling about it, than does codependent caretaking.

Try not to place any blame for your problem either on yourself or on others. Take responsibility for your part in the process, without blaming yourself or regretting the past. You could not know then what you know now, and what you now know is a result of your disease. Everything that happened to you and that will happen to you is part of your personal learning process. Looking back to the past is not productive. Looking forward to the future, while providing hope, can also be counterproductive if you are not living in the present. Granted, at this time in the present you may have too much pain to want to live each moment. Escaping into the past or wanting to be in the future may function as an anesthetic for the moment, but try not to get addicted to time-jumping. The lesson for you to learn is happening right now. The longer it takes to learn it, the more pain you will feel. The more you try to externalize the pain, the more negativity you will create for yourself. It is difficult to heal when you are surrounded by negative thoughts and feelings. It is impossible to move on when you are obsessed with the blame game. This becomes a waste of valuable life time, and a prolongation of your dis-ease.

5. Forgiving

Begin by forgiving your illness for creating your pain. This may sound strange or even impossible, but it is necessary. Forgive any part of yourself that is in any way responsible for it. For example if you have smoked heavily all your life and you now have lung cancer, forgive yourself for being a smoker. Forgive the part of you—your addiction—that led to the vulnerability for this particular disease. You do not have to forgive your lungs—they have worked as well as they could and did not choose to have continual smoke in them. Once you have taken responsibility for the smoking that led to your illness, you can easily forgive the society you grew up in, which reinforced the idea of it, and the tobacco manufacturers, who did not force but did encourage you; and you can also forgive the medical establishment for not producing a cure. You can also forgive your family, if it is relevant. That is, if they were also heavy smokers who sabotaged your attempts to quit.

If you are reluctant to forgive, consider the alternative. You are most likely angry and even hating the causes of your illness. Anger and hatred are feeding your weak ego and inhibiting your development of self-love. Even if these negative emotions are not turned against yourself, they are projections of you and will then rebound against the love of yourself. It is very difficult, if not impossible, to love yourself when you are feeling incessant anger and hate. Your behavior is often based on your feelings, and you cannot behave lovingly when you are angry. Usually you will want to act destructively toward those about whom you have negative feelings. These destructive actions then boomerang back to influence the way you feel about your Self. For this reason forgiveness is a necessary step. The luxury of hating, desiring retribution or revenge, and being constantly angry, is something you cannot afford, especially when you are trying to heal. The act of truly forgiving allows you to move past the unfairness, the injustice, the craziness of it all, and constructively move along with your life. You can only be your best when you are emotionally clean. Forgiveness is a major step in your cleansing process.

6. Appreciating

It may be difficult to find things to appreciate when you are in the midst of a painful and debilitating disease. If you are locked up in negativity, it will be impossible to appreciate anything. If you have followed the previous problem-solving steps, you have already discovered that there are a great many wonderful and positive things going on, even though your disease may be killing you. If you are learning anything new, appreciate that your condition has led you to the place where new knowledge is occurring. Your disease can and will (if you let it) teach you many things about yourself. It will teach you the importance of all the parts of your totality, and it will help you perceive the relationship between all these aspects and the integrated whole that is you. You may be discovering that parts of yourself you once considered unimportant have now become critically important. Your illness may be teaching you tolerance, patience, flexibility, and the real meaning of life. Certainly it will provide you with the opportunity to experience these virtues. When you are ill, you will easily know what your priorities are, and you will be better able to separate what is truly meaningful from what is superficial or irrelevant. The Doing model has taught you to value the externals and has never helped you learn to Be. Now, when you are sick, you will have the time to practice Being. You have been forced to slow down, to think, to take care of yourself. These are some of the necessary conditions for Being.

You have not chosen this, but that is irrelevant because you can still take advantage of the conditions surrounding your diseased state that can be of benefit to your growth and change. You can appreciate that there are positive benefits hidden along the painful course of the process. You can appreciate that you are in a new place and are able to learn new things. All of this is extremely difficult and not what you might choose to do, *if you had the choice.* But since you do not, and you are here in this state, you can choose either to remain fearful and lonely or to search for some positive benefits.

When you are sick, you can see very clearly the people around you who really care about you. Often these loving ones will tell you how they really feel about you, which they may not be able to do when you are well. Appreciate the love that is being given to you. When you are loved, you are receiving a wonderful gift from someone else—a gift that has to be freely given, and is not meaningful if it is demanded or expected. Recognize that you are lovable in your vulnerable state— maybe even more lovable than when you are strong and healthy. Be grateful for the things about yourself that are working toward your self-healing. Honor your sense of humor, as nothing will help you heal faster than the ability to laugh with others and at yourself. Appreciate the things you have lost, such as your facade of perfection, your need to be strong, your fear of vulnerability, your stoic nature, your guilt, your codependent tendencies, and appreciate your diminished weak ego. These are wonderful things to lose, and your disease has put you in the place where you can lose them. Appreciate the process, the learning, those who are helping and loving you, and above all appreciate yourself. If you have learned to love yourself, be thankful. If you have not yet, but want to, value the wanting, and act *as if* you loved yourself. This becomes a habit that turns into a reality. Finally, appreciate that you are still able to practice appreciation, here and now, in your painful place.

7. Rewarding

If ever rewarding were important in the problem-solving process, it is now, in your diseased state. This is the time to be supremely kind to your Self. This is not the time to deny yourself small pleasures or to be hard on yourself. If you are treating yourself badly, recognize that this is because you are the product of unhealthy training. You are good and you deserve to be rewarded. You are probably in pain and you need to do whatever it takes to alleviate your pain. Necessary pain, which cannot be avoided, is an inseparable part of life; unnecessary pain, which can be alleviated or avoided, teaches you nothing, but feeds the weak ego. Reward yourself for surviving your pain. These rewards can be anything that makes you feel better, or they can be things that you have previously denied yourself because you did not feel deserving. Your disease has taught you that you deserve to feel better. You may have also learned that it is impossible to be perfect and that if you delay gratification until you are perfect, you will never receive it. Gratify yourself now. Be loving, kind, concerned, and aware of your own Self. Allow others to be the same with you. In your hour of need know that you have great worth, are of supreme value, and are loved. Begin that love with yourself. Then continue by acting lovingly toward yourself at all times. You will heal, sometimes miraculously, if you know that you are worth healing.

Do not forget to reward those around you who are trying to help. It is not their fault that they may not be able to "fix" or "cure" you, but the fact that they care deserves thanks. Kind words, pleasant smiles, loving touches, and being considerate and thoughtful are powerful rewards for your caretakers. The results of being kind toward those who are helping you will become rewards for yourself. You will be creating a loving system and you will benefit. You will heal faster in a loving environment, your emotions will be easier to deal with, your mind and thoughts will be peaceful and clear, and your spirits will soar. The loved and rewarded you will not succumb to the inherent negativity that exists in the state of being dis-eased, but will rise above it and expand and enhance all around you and, most especially, the totality of the integrated you. In spite of your disease, or perhaps because of it, you will learn to become eased. You will know now about Being and you will know how little is really important, but exactly how important it is. When you reward the important, meaningful things in your life, you create more of them. You enrich, enhance, and expand your life and well-being. And these are the most meaningful rewards of all.

All of life is rehearsal for our death.

—WALTER "BUZZ" O'CONNELL

XIII ⌐ Loss and Death

It may be the ultimate irony that we spend the first part of our lives becoming attached, in order to survive, and we spend the last part of our lives learning to detach, in order to die. We begin life being connected, and this connection, the umbilical cord, must be severed in order for us to exist in this world. The infant arrives, helpless, vulnerable, and desperately seeking the connection it has lost. As part of the normal development process the baby begins attaching to Mother psychologically before the age of one. In doing so he or she is developing a secure base from which to venture out and explore the world. This process of attachment continues throughout the next few decades, first to others and then to things. We cannot survive, develop, learn, and grow without being attached. Our spirits perceive it as a replacement for the connection we constantly yearn for.

Unfortunately attachments to things or to others are not true spiritual connections, and these attachments lead to our problems. It may now be obvious (from reading the preceding chapters) that all our problems are in some form the result of our attachments. They can be perceived as fulfilling our quest for belonging and connection, but they are probably most accurately understood as reflections of our degrees of neediness— our insecurities. However, there is no way to circumvent this process: We cannot learn to detach unless we first become attached, and we cannot avoid the detachment process, no matter how much we resist. The most fundamental truth about life is that we will die—we will all become detached from our bodies, our Selves, life as we know it, and the people and things we have attached ourselves to.

Defining Death

Death is not the enemy; it is the supreme completion. It is the culmination of all problem-solving abilities, and the ultimate letting go. Because we know we are going to die, to lose others to death, to eventually detach from all externals, we have a lifelong incentive to practice our letting-go skills. Life may be considered a rehearsal for the real show—our death and afterlife, whatever that may entail. All our denial, all our fears and clinging to the externals of this world, all our possessions and attributes, our will and our strength, all that we know and value will not stop our death. We are forced to learn to detach because, no matter how hard we try to resist this education, we will ultimately receive it. We may choose, as Dylan Thomas wrote, not to "go gentle into that good night," but no matter how we do it, we must still go. This awareness may paradoxically be our greatest comfort. Without this certainty we would have very little reason to begin the painful process of detachment or even fully to appreciate our attachments, our lives. Recognizing and facing this reality brings meaning to our lives and soothes, by justifying, our pain. In this way all loss may be perceived as preparation for the final one, the loss of the Self.

The Necessity of Loss

Everything external to ourselves we will lose. Some of these losses we may perceive as positive. For example when we lose our vulnerabilities or fears, our phobias or loneliness, we view this as good. Most of our losses, however, we consider negative. When we are deprived of someone we love, either intentionally (when he leaves us) or inadvertently (when he dies), we mourn and bewail the loss. When we lose our money or our possessions, we usually feel cheated, unlucky, or resentful. And if we try to lose ourselves by engaging in self-destructive behavior, we become truly alienated. These negative consequences are caused by our belief systems, which in turn come from the model of how the world *should* work. This model teaches us that we should be able to control our lives and therefore our losses. Our concepts of good and bad, right and wrong, positive and negative, are also derived from our model for life. It implies that loss is bad, wrong, negative, unnecessary, and to be avoided if possible.

From a spiritual perspective all loss is necessary in order for growth to occur. The soul perceives loss as the beginning of something new rather than the ending of something good. Recognizing that we need to experience it does not mean that we can alleviate or escape from the pain it produces. Indeed we will judge the extent of our deprivation by the amount of pain we suffer. We can more easily accept that loss is necessary when we remember that life is not fair and that it is often painful. When we become stuck in trying to deny or disprove these basic truths, we are unable to see that loss is a needed precursor to change. When we are fighting against losing, it becomes impossible for us to understand the critical role it plays in our development process. Without these realizations we will be unable to understand the concept of rehearsing for our death by living to our fullest potential. Instead we will be imprisoned by the past, before the loss occurred, and in denial of the future; we will be unable to live in the reality of the present. This will lead to alienation from our souls and will prevent the great healer—hope—from developing. When we choose to fight against or try to deny the pain of our detachment, we lose much more than we can realize: We lose our relationships with our inner selves, our souls, and our spirits. In so doing we lose our feeling of connectedness with God.

The Training About Loss

We have not been taught to perceive loss as a part of our life process. Our society does not in any way view this concept as positive or important. Our culture assumes that when we lose, it is our fault, and if we do so consistently, we are defined as failures. The Doing model does not deal with either our spirituality or our souls; indeed it does not begin to deal with our relationship with God. The primary goal of the model is worldly success, which translates to fame and fortune. The values derived from it are determined by external and socially desired outcomes. We are taught to value appearing to be successful much more than we value really being balanced, whole, and spiritually alive. We are not taught that everything we really need we already have and that we must look inside to find it. Instead we are taught that everything we need is external to the self and that we must work hard to gain it. Therefore when we lose, which we will, we must be doing something wrong. Perhaps just the opposite is true: when we lose, we are being forced into doing something "right," to go inside to find what we need. Some of our most difficult and painful losses may occur when we resist this process of learning about the internal self, of relating to the spirit and soul, of becoming detached in order to begin to be connected.

The Myth of Connection

When we are born, we instinctively know that we have been disconnected from something important, and as we develop, we slowly come to realize that we have a buried but basic need to find this connection again. We come to recognize that something is missing and we feel a strong sense of loss, deep within our unknown selves. Early on we discover that this emptiness within, this heartfelt loneliness, is somewhat assuaged by other relationships. Because we yearn to be connected again but do not know how or even to what, we begin by attaching to Mother as a means of stopping the pain. And this works for a short while. As we grow, we discover that we can also attach to things to stop the pain. Most of us become addicts to the external world—the life of luxuries and adoration, success and recognition. All this also stops the pain, for a while. The more we turn to the externals of life to satisfy our needs, the less we seem to feel that deep yearning inside. The Western model teaches us to do more, to have more, in order to feel better. It reinforces the idea that we have a right to be happy and it defines happiness as the acquisition of things and people. We all know what the "good life" looks like and we think that this is what we are yearning for.

If we are really unlucky, we may even achieve society's definition of happiness. How very quickly we then discover that this is not what we were yearning for, that the emptiness and loneliness inside have not disappeared but rather have begun to haunt us at the most inappropriate of times. We have faithfully followed the model, we have achieved worldly success, but internally we are not happy or at peace and we still feel disconnected. We think that the model cannot be wrong; therefore we must be wrong. We are unlucky because now we have developed the facade that everyone else desires and strives for, and this false front stops the true self—the unhappy, disillusioned self, the lost spirit, and the distant soul—from being known, even to ourselves. Furthermore we must hide from ourselves in order to maintain this facade of success, in order to continue to fool ourselves and others. We are truly unlucky because we have lost more than we have ever gained, and these external things that we so valued have now imprisoned us. They are the stuff of the weak ego, which is the antithesis of self-esteem. Really knowing and loving the Self opens the door to the deep self, the God within.

Unnecessary Loss

The important losses in life are the ones that we cannot control. These are the ones that have real meaning for us and create deep pain when they are gone. They can be defined as the ones that are connected to our internal selves and that help us develop integrity, character, and true strength. Most of us have very little idea of what they actually are, unless we lose everything or are approaching the end of our lives. Then we quickly recognize their importance and grieve their loss. Unfortunately most of us have not been taught to recognize the worth and appreciate the possession of such things while we still have them. They are not the things, status, goods, money, or valuable possessions that most of us spend our lives accumulating. Ironically the stuff *of* life is rarely the stuff *in* life. The things that we possess, and that often come to possess us, are rarely necessary for our internal lives and usually lack real meaning once we come to own them. In spite of this we worry about acquiring such things and we fear losing them. When we do lose them, and we always do, we discover that we have not really lost much. These losses—the unnecessary and secondary ones—are not constructive or beneficial for our growth and development; in reality they function as substitutions for or diversions from the search for meaning and connection. The losses that will teach us, those that are important and necessary, are not in our control. They can most simply be defined as our most meaningful connections.

A wonderful paradox here is that when we think that we have everything to lose (as defined by society's standards) may be when we really have little of value to lose. And when we feel we have nothing left to lose may be when we actually begin to connect to that within us that has real value, that which may have previously been lost to us. There are several relevant examples of this in recent highly publicized criminal trials concerning well-known, successful defendants who had "everything"—as defined by the model—and yet were obviously internally suffering and in great pain. Their interior emptiness and lack of self-esteem was evident from their stories and their crimes. In all cases society defined them as unqualified successes, possessors of fame, fortune, status, and the so-called good life. But no one asked, until too late, how they perceived themselves. As their trials progressed, it became evident that all of them were in some way "lost souls." Their facades crumbled in front of the world, and their foundations were seen to be weak and not secure. Their stories are classic examples of following the Doing model, catering to the weak ego and denying the development of self-esteem. If any of them had possessed self-esteem, they could not have been involved in their predicaments. If any of them had been internally secure, they would not have consistently acted on or reacted to their insecurities.

Perhaps now, when they have lost everything of worldly value, they can begin the real work of finding themselves. At the very least their crimes and trials, their imprisonments and humiliations, have provided them with the opportunity to discover that there is no escape from the Self. Perhaps now they have learned from their painful experiences that we take ourselves with us wherever we go and we cannot hide from who we really are. All the money in the world, all the fame and trappings of luxury, are not worth anything if we become disconnected from our souls—if we lose our attachment to God. We can all learn from their painful stories.

Finding the Connection

There are no shortcuts to our interiors; there is no way to search inside without feeling loss and pain. There is simply no path to connectedness that begins and ends with the externals. Our necessary losses are those that break the facade and cause us to begin the search for the Self. Often these losses lead to the discovery of our goodness and the realization that what we all yearn for exists within. These losses teach us that we are humble, vulnerable, tenuous, limited, and in spite of all this we are good and have great worth. Our goodness comes from God and exists even when our actions deny it. It only ceases when we repeatedly turn away from it and deliberately try to do evil. Evil exists, but it is not what drives most of us to hurt ourselves or others. Most of us do bad things because we are insecure rather than evil. Our insecurities cause us pain, and we then inflict our pain upon those around us. Our society reinforces these insecurities and the development of the weak ego; many of our actions reflect a too-faithful adherence to a sick system, a dysfunctional model, one that only values achieving goals and having external possessions. Fortunately we do not have to resort to destructive behavior before we realize what is really needed. We do not have to wait to fall or be pushed off the model; we can jump off whenever we choose. The losses we sustain in our lives are lessons that provide new options; they are forced detachments from externals that provide us with the possibility of getting where we need to be. They function as a way of helping us recover from our emotional addictions. They are life's messengers of the need to let go.

The Process of Loss

No matter how old we may be, we have already sustained great loss in our lives. The infant attaches to mother and wails each time she leaves. We quickly lose our infancy and reluctantly enter childhood. When we become threatened or feel insecure, we try to regress to a safer time, and find we cannot. The child attaches to the safety of home and cries when he must begin school. Friends leave, parents are discovered to be less than invincible, we grow out of our favorite toys and clothes—we even grow out of our own bodies. We lose our identities in order to belong with our peers, and we once again lose our feeling of security in the world. When we become afraid, we try to regress and find we cannot. We reluctantly leave childhood to enter adolescence. Here we lose our belonging-ingness with our family, our identities as protected children, our illusions that the world is fair, just, and safe, and the adoration of our friends and loved ones. We become afraid, try to regress, and find that we cannot. As difficult as adolescence is, we become familiar with it, and go reluctantly, often screaming and resisting, into adulthood.

In this adult stage we lose any remaining illusions about how the world should work. We lose people we love and need, we lose material possessions, and we usually lose ourselves. In this process we lose our defense mechanisms or our energy trying to keep them. Many of us depart from our traditional religious beliefs, our certainty that God exists, our connectedness to our own spirits and souls, and our emotional balance. We certainly lose at least one person we love, either to death or to a lack of caring. We lose our identities again, we try to regress to a safe place, and discover that we cannot, for there is no such thing as a safe place. We discover once more that life is unfair, justice is an illusion, and that we do not know what we want—what we are yearning for. We find that no matter what we try to do—work more, drink more, take drugs, have love affairs, enter politics, do volunteer work, preach love and peace, become entrepreneurs, whatever—we cannot escape from the loneliness within, the quiet but insistent yearning to belong, to be whole, to be connected.

We have finally arrived at the place where we are ready to rediscover what we have hidden all along. We are ready for that deep, dark, mysterious trip into the unknown—into the interior of the Self. We cannot go backward, we cannot stay where we are (we are too miserable), and the only option is to go forward. Our deprivations have left us confused, frustrated, bored, vulnerable, and afraid. We are ripe for change. We are now ready to learn. We are reluctant students, but we have exercised all other options. Our spirituality is calling us and, with great trepidation, we move forward.

Detaching

The process we are encountering, if we are lucky (bruised, scared, and unsure), is the loss of attachment, the beginning of detachment. What we are about to lose—the attachment to externals, to the facade, to the illusions and expectations of the self, the addiction to the weak ego—is nothing compared with what we are about to receive. We are on the threshold of losing our perception of the self in order to satisfy that old yearning—the connection to the Whole. We are about to die symbolically in order to be reborn. There are worse things than physically dying: If we lose our relationship with our soul, or if we lose trust in our own "guts," our intuitions and our instincts, we truly become spiritually dead and this is a far greater loss than physical death.

The spirit can be perceived in the relationship with the Self; spirituality requires the ability to know and trust ourselves. The soul can be understood as the part of ourselves that knows everything and integrates all in a constructive, meaningful manner. Thus the spirit relates and the soul interrelates. Neither subscribes to the values taught by the Doing model. The soul does not judge, compete, compare, or label. Everything that we are, that we have done, all our actions, intentions, and feelings, are food for the soul. Everything in our lives becomes necessary to the soul, in order for us to reach the next level, to learn what we have to know, and then to let it all go. The soul is not as concerned with the content of our lives as it is with the process. Therefore losses are not viewed as tragic but rather as inspirational and critical parts of the life process.

The weak ego is not the enemy of the soul but rather an important adversary, which functions to provide us with choices and options; thus it is a necessary part of our being. Becoming soulful does not mean the loss of the weak ego; becoming spiritual does not mean that we strive for perfection. The interior of ourselves is much more forgiving than the exterior. The interior is where God resides within us—this is where our goodness exists. It is here that we satisfy our great yearning and it is only here that we can discover the reality of our true selves. We tend to perceive this journey inward as awful; what we find when we are forced to travel is that it is full of awe. The great mysteries of our lives are always with us. If they were revealed early on, before we fully attached and were not yet ready to begin detaching, they would not be meaningful. Our life meaning comes from this process of self-discovery. The journey to the God within is a requirement, a necessary process, which allows us to recover from the pain of our losses. This journey to the Self ultimately means the loss of the self. This process is one of the great mysteries and another paradox, full of wonder, fear, and pain.

Pain and Loss

As mentioned, there are far worse things than physical death. Anyone who has experienced severe chronic pain knows this. Those subjected to intolerable abuse, terror, or situations of victimization frequently yearn for death as a release. The hope for change functions as a buffer against pain and fear. As long as we know or believe that what we are experiencing will end, and end in a positive way, we can survive and cope. When we have no conception of an ending, when we fear that there is no light at the end of our tunnel, we despair and long for release, even if it means no longer surviving. In some ways emotional pain can be worse than physical or bodily pain. It can be devastating in its intensity and debilitating by its persistence. For those who have never experienced severe emotional pain, it is hard to imagine that something unseen can hurt that much. It is hard to believe that our feelings can create such havoc inside us, especially when the outside (the body) is not injured. Emotional pain indicates the depth and intensity of our soul and spirit, also unseen, but existing nonetheless.

Emotional pain is always about loss, and loss is always related to death—if not physical, then spiritual, metaphysical, or psychological death. Loss causes a shock to the unseen system, in the same manner that physical pain shocks the body. This prepares the way for change to occur. Metaphorically it wakes us up with a slap, and then waits to see how we will respond. It provides us with new choices, often those that we may not have been aware of before we were in pain, and it causes us to try something unknown, to charter unmapped territory, to take risks. Scary stuff, but critical for the process of life and death.

Taking the Risk

Everything we have done had first to be done once, and this meant taking a risk. Our life, when chartered on a spiritual level, would appear to be a series of emerging and retreating actions, of exploring the unknown (courage), making it known (comfort), and venturing off into the unknown once again (growth). Each time we venture, we discover that we need to take less and less with us. Our possessions, which once provided us with security and comfort, now seem to weigh us down. As we get older, we travel lighter and lighter, need fewer material possessions to make us content, and we begin to care less and less about more and more. We have reached the age of detachment and are truly preparing to die. If we have learned anything about ourselves along the journey, this process feels natural and quite comfortable. The more we have explored our own interiors, the more chances we have had to encounter the God within. If this has occurred, then we know that death is simply going home, and not to be feared in the least.

If we have spent our lives resisting the lessons that have been consistently provided for us, if we have ignored the teachings of our pain, fear, and weaknesses, and if we are obsessed with protecting our external self from the internal one, we are going to be terrified at the idea of death. If we have only practiced the weak ego and followed the Doing model, we will be unable to see life as rehearsal and will fear the ending of "all there is." Our losses will have been perceived as woundings of our physical and emotional selves, to be healed, avenged, and forgotten. When we choose to take the other path, the one inside, away from the externals, the one on the Being model, we will begin by loving our Self as much as anyone or anything else. We will next discover that this love flows out of us and into others. When we risk knowing our dark sides, and bring them into the light, we meet our souls.

Another great paradox: Our souls do not live in the places that we consider strong and wonderful; they live in our dark sides, along with our fears and vulnerabilities. Our souls, which become the greatest strength about us (they alone survive our physical death), live in that part of ourselves that we believe lacks strength. Our dark sides are where we hide the garbage of our lives, until we become fearful of exposing the rot and stink. We cannot expose this most fearful part easily or quickly. But when we do, we discover that there is nothing to be afraid of—all is known, all is clear, and the fear exists not here but in the barriers and defenses that have kept us away. It is impossible to know the Self and be at the same time alienated from the dark side, the home of the soul. Our losses provide the lamps along the path, and our death provides the reason for going on the journey to the God within while we are still alive.

XIV ∾ Problem-Solving Loss and Death

1. Accepting

As usual this will most likely be the most difficult of the seven steps for you to take. Accepting the idea that you will die sounds ridiculously simple; of course you know that you will die sometime. *But not now,* a voice inside your head usually adds. And this is what makes the process not simple and not easy. Dying is something for later, and there is still too much to do right now. *Besides,* you might astutely answer, *I need to be living in the present and not worrying about the future, right?* Except that you are always dying, and death has been a constant companion throughout your life. Physically, parts of you are dying all the time—skin and brain cells, liver and stomach cells—dying off and being replaced. You are not the same person you were ten years ago, and certainly you are not who you were as a child. Those past beings are lost, or physically dead, although parts of them remain as memories and feelings.

Everything you have lost can be conceived of as dead for you now. Your life has consisted of one change after another, one loss following another, small deaths at all times. Yet you are surviving and you are probably not afraid of what you have lost in your past. You may even be able to understand how all these small deaths have allowed you to become what you are now. Once you can look past the content of your life and view it as process, you will better be able to accept your ultimate physical death. If you can see your losses as rehearsals for the final (as we know it) letting go, you will be better able to face your death without fear or anxiety. And you will have no difficulty accepting that the only constructive way to prepare for the unavoidable release of physiological life is to live fully and completely. Use all your experiences, your pains and fears, your frustrations and mistakes, and especially your losses to help pave the path toward letting go gracefully. By living as much as possible in the moment, you will become prepared for your death.

2. Letting Go

The actual letting go of your human existence is not in your control, and rightly so, because you cannot understand the interrelationship of the whole, or know what purpose your life has in the great pattern. When depressed souls try to take control of their deaths by committing suicide, they may be disrupting something much more complex than they could ever conceptualize. Or they may just be taking the shortcut, the easy way out, and if so, they will most likely have to learn their necessary lessons on some other plane. There are no shortcuts to the important things, and there is probably no shortcut to death. There may indeed be mitigating circumstances for suicide with the old or the critically ill, but certainly not for those who are healthy, young, foolish, or afraid. Letting go refers not to the ending of our existence but to the detaching from the detriments to the journey inward.

Let go of the idea that death is failure, or fearful, or a complete ending. Let go of any notions that you are immortal and that death will not happen to you. Let go of the idea that you should be brave or stoical or fight death when it comes. Let go of "should." You do not have to get rid of anything—possessions, faults, fears, or others—until it is the natural time to do so. If you are truly stuck in coveting the externals or if you are excessive with your fears or anxiety, please get professional help. You do not have to be in such unnecessary pain. Once again let go of the idea that you have to be perfect in order to be worthy to die and be with God. You will be forgiven, your goodness is already a given, and going to God is not difficult. The going-inside-yourself is far more difficult in the beginning. This journey inside will be impossible unless you are first able to let go of the idea that what you want, need, and yearn for is to be found in externals. Once you have released yourself from society's seductive messages concerning happiness and success, once you have jumped off the Doing model, you will find it easier to let go of the myths and illusions of the weak ego.

Let go of the idea that you will not have to let go. Begin the process by remembering all the things that you have already lost, all the changes you have made, and the fact that basically you can manage. Let go of the mistaken idea that happiness is a right, that life should be easy and comfortable, and that loss is unbearable. You can do it, you have been doing it, and being a problem solver rather than a problem responder means that letting go is a natural, if painful, part of the process of your life.

This process is similar to detaching, and yet there is a major difference between letting go and spiritually detaching. The first is a conscious process and only somewhat within your control; the latter is not. You can often choose what you will keep and what you will let go of, but you cannot consciously choose when you will spiritually detach from something or someone. Perhaps the best example of this occurs with those you love. You may be forced to let go of someone you love—your child, your parent, your lover—but you cannot choose to be emotionally or spiritually detached from him or her. This spiritual detachment will occur when you are ready to die. You can let go of external things and your weak ego as you live, but detaching from them is a natural and unconscious process that occurs when you become ready to die. Forcing this detachment process, trying not to care in order to avoid the pain, is an artificial process, born of defenses and denial. This does not add to your development and completion, but instead blocks them. When you are dying, the detachment occurs as a normal part of the death process. The paradox here is that the more attached you are, the more that you live life and love your Self and others, the more involved you are in the moment, the easier it is naturally to detach when the time comes. This timing is not in your control and therefore not your responsibility.

3. Expressing Feelings

By now you are probably aware that you cannot control your feelings except for the choice of how you feel about yourself. All other emotions are frequent and spontaneous occurrences dependent upon forces outside of your control. The way that you choose to feel about yourself is critical in determining how you will live your life and go to your death. If you cannot love yourself and recognize your own worth, how can you possibly believe that your life has meaning and value? Consequently your feelings about dying will be painful and difficult to deal with. We now clearly recognize that humans go through stages in dealing with loss and death, and that these stages are composed of feelings of anger, denial, and sadness before the stage of acceptance is reached. These feelings, while painful to deal with and to observe, are necessary for the process. You will feel anger and you will want to regress back to a safer place whenever you confront a major loss, whether it be of the self, of a beloved, or of something you value. Express these feelings, get them out so that they will not block you from your progress. The idea that you must be stoic and brave or in other words not express what you are feeling is born from our model, which values appearance above reality. This is a dangerous concept because in trying to appear to be something you are not, you risk alienating yourself from your soul.

Expressing your anger, particularly when you are confronting death, does not mean taking it out on others. It does not mean going out of control, although this may be how you feel. It does mean that you talk about what you feel, if only to yourself. If you cannot trust yourself or if you are afraid of what you are feeling, by all means seek help. There are many supportive and understanding others who can relate to what you are feeling; after all, what you are dealing with is a normal human expression. The same holds true with your sadness. You do not have to become severely depressed in order to deal with your situation. Expressing your sadness is the surest way to avoid becoming blocked by depression. You have the right to be sad, for you are losing something of great value. You also have the right to be afraid. Whenever you lose something, you are at risk for facing the unknown. And when you do so, you will always be fearful. Express yourself, be human, be angry and afraid and sad. At this moment these feelings are the reality of your life. They will not always be so, and you will get to a different place, but at this moment you need to confront them.

4. Taking Responsibility

You have probably heard many times that in order to die well, you must live well. This is only possible when you manage to take responsibility for your life. It sounds so easy, but it is one of the rarest things that can be seen—a person who is totally responsible for his or her own life. This is so rare most likely because we have been trained by a model that does not teach responsibility as a critical component of life. Instead society teaches you to delegate, deny, defer, and blame instead of accepting what you are responsible for. You did not ask to be born, you certainly did not deserve all the adversity and unfairness you have received, and you cannot control the externals of your life. But you can control what you do with what you have received; this is where your responsibility lies.

Everything that happens to you, no matter why it happens, presents a choice for you to make. Your life is made up of these multiple choices. When you choose to do the best you can instead of questioning why it happened, when you shoulder the difficulties and move ahead instead of blaming others or defending yourself, when you accept that your life is not fair and that you are not perfect and you still choose to keep going, to be courageous, to be a hero, then you are taking responsibility. When you choose to love yourself, flawed and unknowing as you are, and you also choose to love others, knowing that you risk great pain in doing so, then you are living to the best of your ability. If you give up the quest for happiness as your ultimate life goal and replace it with the search for inner peace, then you are allowing your life to be meaningful. All these choices require an awareness of what you can and cannot control, and of what you are responsible for. Remember, you can only control your feelings about yourself and your behaviors based on these feelings. And they are ultimately the only things you are responsible for. These two things determine the quality of your life and the outcome of your being. Doing them as well as you can, which means really loving yourself as well as risking to love others, and taking full responsibility for your actions, no matter what others do, is a lifetime occupation. Can you think of any better way to live your life?

5. Forgiving

Begin by forgiving yourself for being mortal, for having to learn by losing, and for having to die. This may sound absurd—of course you are human and therefore must die—but your training has allowed you to deny or defer this truth. It has also led you to believe that you have failed when you lose and that you are weak when you feel unsure. Forgive yourself when you are afraid of what you must lose in order to learn. Forgive yourself for feeling sad and insecure when you have lost your illusions of safety and security in the world. Above all, forgive yourself for not knowing everything, and stop punishing yourself for being imperfect, for making mistakes, and for being wrong. You must forgive yourself in order to know your own soul, for your soul does not judge. In order to become soulful, you must suspend judgment, and you need to begin with your Self before you can forgive others. Forgiving others is the surest way to becoming spiritual, for your spirituality exists in this ability, even if you do not always understand the process. Your intuition is in closer connection with your spirituality than is your reason.

The Doing model has taught you to value thinking above feeling; the Being model teaches the opposite. Quite often you have done things that were rationally labeled wrong but instinctively felt right. Frequently you have done things that were cognitively right, but intuitively you knew they were wrong. Forgive yourself for being confused and for not always knowing what was the best thing to do. Especially forgive yourself for the things that you have done that you were clear about. The best you can be at any time is when you are trying to do your best, as you determine it to be at that moment.

You do not have to suffer for or forgive yourself for things that were out of your control, as long as you have taken responsibility for the things that you could control. Absolve yourself, but do not stop learning from your mistakes. Forgiveness does not mean that you have to forget; it is in the remembering of how you feel about yourself that you learn about what works for you, what allows you to feel good about yourself, and what does not. This awareness leads to change, and this leads to your connection with your soul and the God within you. If God, understanding all, can forgive all, how can you not try to do the same?

6. Appreciating

Another paradox: The more you appreciate something, the less pain you will experience when you lose it or when you die. Appreciation is a big part of living your life to the fullest. It is ironic that when you try to control, or keep, or become possessive of things or others, you stop appreciating them. Being thankful works best when you recognize the transitory nature of everything you love and value. All these things are on loan to you—even your own life is a short-term loan—and if you can appreciate everything you have when you have it, you will find it easier to let it go, which you must do. And the more that you can appreciate these precious things, the less you will grieve when they are no longer yours.

You have not been trained to be appreciative because you have been taught to possess and to measure your worth by the number of possessions you own. You have learned to fight pain and to deny death. Being appreciative will not stop all pain, but it will lessen the necessary pains of life and help you to resist the unnecessary ones. You will know that you have learned the process of being thankful when you are able to appreciate the lessons your losses have taught you, even when you are in great pain from them. Begin to learn this difficult process by thinking of all the things you can appreciate right now. Make a list of them; you will probably be surprised by the length of your list. You have probably been taught to make lists of all the things you want but do not have. Reverse this and make lists of all the things you have but have not yet realized you want. One way to define *appreciation* is "wanting the things you already have." It can also be defined as "the recognition that you are lucky to have them and the awareness that you will not always be this lucky."

Give thanks for being you—there is no one else exactly like you. Give thanks for having your own life story—there is no other one exactly like yours. Appreciate your ability to love and be loved; this is one of your greatest gifts from God. And always remember to appreciate the fact that you are trying your best, especially when the outcome is difficult and causes you pain. Try to appreciate that you are always learning and that you are struggling to make sense of this crazy world. If you feel that you have nothing else to appreciate, you can always be thankful that you have survived, in spite of your difficulties and problems. Know that the more thankful you can be, the less difficult your life will be. The more you can appreciate the present, the less you will have to fear in the future, or feel guilt about in the past. By appreciating the moment as it occurs, by looking for something positive instead of allowing the negative to overwhelm you, you will be fully living the present. This is all you really have in your control, and this is what your life is made of—present moments in which you choose to be either positive or negative. Appreciating gives you courage and allows you to endure the hard times. En-courage yourself by being always thankful.

7. Rewarding

Many people die with regret for the things they have not done that they really wanted to do for themselves. Rewarding yourself is about doing these things so that you do not have to die with regret. If you can begin by loving yourself and continue by taking responsibility for your own life, then it is easier to appreciate what you are and what you have done, and even easier still to reward yourself. If you cannot love yourself, it will be almost impossible to feel worthy of self-recognition. Accepting rewards from others is nice, but it is not the same thing as rewarding yourself, because only you know what you really need and want. It is up to you to take care of these needs and wants. Society may have brainwashed you into believing that you must wait for others to reward you and that you have no right to give yourself pleasure, but you now know that society's model does not work. It focuses its attention on external rewards, and these do not satisfy internal needs. The Doing model perpetuates the myth of happiness as the ultimate goal, and in so doing creates a great deal of unhappiness. If your goal is peace of mind and a reconnection with your soul (God within), rewarding yourself will bring you closer to your goal.

You can learn what you have not been taught by taking a little time every day just for yourself. Your soul lives in a quiet place, and to know your soul requires solitude and moments of peace. Reward yourself by allowing this to occur on a regular basis. Your spirit lives with those you love and who love you. Reward yourself by being in loving and supportive environments as much as possible. You deserve to be well treated; reward yourself by treating yourself well. Say kind things to yourself, give yourself little treats, enjoy something in this moment. Pay attention to what your body wants and needs, and reward yourself by fulfilling these needs. Do something nice for yourself each and every day, and know that you deserve it.

You are full of wonder, full of love, full of great mystery and joy. When you take good care of yourself, all these things appear for you to experience and know. The final paradox is that when you recognize all the beauty inside yourself and you know the wonder and joy, the love and caring, that are you, you will be more than ready to let go, detach, and go with

God. Then you will not be going to the unknown, but instead will be returning to the familiar, the known. You will simply be going home. You will bless God, and God will bless you. Can there be any greater reward?

⌒ Epilogue

You may have already discovered the relationship between the seven problem-solving steps and self-esteem. Using the steps to solve your difficulties will naturally result in increasing your sense of self-worth; the steps will help you break down the barriers of the weak ego and allow you to perceive where your training has gone wrong. These outcomes are not accidental; it is not coincidence that they are related to the process of developing self-love. There just are not that many positive things to learn in order to live well and discover the meaning of life. There are, however, far too many negatives to distract you on your journey. You may believe that learning and using the positive seems so difficult, whereas living in the negative seems so easy. Paradoxically the opposite is true. Many of your problems will be solved when you recognize this.

When you use the seven steps, and really work them thoroughly, you will lose your fear of always having difficulties to deal with. You will begin to think of your problems as challenges, and you will know that, whatever happens, you can cope. You will have realized the purpose for this book. And if you do only this, you will have learned a great deal. But there are other consequences from these steps—outcomes I did not dream of when I began *The Portable Problem Solver*. When you become an active and aware problem solver, when these seven steps become a natural part of your life process, you will become firmly established on the Being model. As you begin to learn how to accept, you will simultaneously be learning how to be. When you let go of the craziness, the Doing model, the myths and illusions and the fears that have dominated your previous existence, you will consciously become involved with Being. As you express your feelings and take responsibility for your share of the difficulties, you will become more real, more sensitive, and more aware of the true meaning for your life. And when you practice forgiving, appreciating, and rewarding, you will be fully living your goodness and you will be creating a positive, nurturing environment for your Self and also for those around you. Therefore if you are tired of always doing and curious about how to be, use these steps. They will take you where you want to be.

But perhaps the most marvelous outcome of all is that the seven problem-solving steps are exactly the ones that develop your spirituality and nurture your soul. The steps teach you to recognize the realities, let go of the myths, cope with the feelings, stop the blame games, and realize, appreciate, and reward the goodness within yourself and others. They teach you what and when to forgive so that you can move on. All of these lessons are also the lessons of spirituality. The process of working the steps will bring you to the discovery of the God within, and this is what will make you soulful.

When you practice the steps, not only are you problem-solving, Being, demonstrating your spirituality, and discovering your soul, but you are concurrently demonstrating love. You are now actively loving. Because love is better defined by your behavior than it is by your feelings, and because how you behave depends on how you feel about yourself, loving your Self will lead to having more love for others. When you actively love, you enhance the world. Perhaps this is more important than making new discoveries, accomplishing great goals, or becoming famous and "successful." The real accomplishments in life, the true successes, the most meaningful discoveries are the internal ones. Therefore you can problem-solve to deal with your difficulties, but in the meantime you will really be doing the work of your life. How wonderful that your newfound abilities can be generalized to all aspects of your being. How fortunate that you can learn seven steps to resolve any difficulty and that at the same time you will be dealing with the most important issues of your life. By the time you read this, you will have discovered that there are things you can do to cope with any difficulty. Now you have discovered that these same things will help you live your life to the fullest; they will allow you to be a pilgrim, angel, and hero of your own destiny. God be with you in your journey to be with God.